The Natural Laws Of Work

How to stay cool, calm and collected in the office

The Natural Laws Of Work

How to stay cool, calm and collected in the office

By Prue Nichols

First published, June 2014

Copyright © Prue Nichols

Prue Nichols has asserted her right under the Copyright, Design and Patent Act 1988 to be identified as the author of this work.

All rights reserved.

Acknowledgments

"Silent gratitude isn't much use to anyone."
— GB Stern

I've wanted to write this book for many years and like everything in life, its creation has been a team effort. I've been blessed to meet many inspirational people on my journey and have many wonderful friends and family who are an infinite source of wisdom and support.

When working in public relations I would particularly like to thank Sasha Martin and Claire Doherty, two hugely talented women who I was lucky to work with and learn from. Also, a thank you to Emma Flack and Helen Fenwick, both mentors for me at Unilever who demonstrated how to do business with a heart.

My holistic training started under the watch of Anna Jeoffroy and Philip Salmon at Energy Works. Thank you – your course changed the direction that my life was taking. I was very lucky to study holistic massage under Katya Langmuir – thank you for having the bar so high and showing me how sacred touch is. A very special thank you to Ali and Elaine at the Nutritional Healing Foundation – your course, many years later, still inspires me and I'm still learning and acting upon your generously shared knowledge.

My KPI friends continue to be a source of great support - thank you Daniel Priestley for creating this community that has shaped my vision and helped make my dream a reality. My designer, Marianne Hartley, who breathes beauty and life into the The Orange Grove. My editor Lorna Howarth at The Write Factor – thank you so much for all your wisdom, as well as all the care and attention you have poured into this project. My wise and trusted friends who have actively supported me during this book writing adventure - Carey, Jessica, Katie, Avni, Danielle, Thao, Leigh and Emily. Thank you, thank you, thank you.

To all my clients - thank you for being part of my life. I've learnt so much from you all and feel so lucky that work never feels like 'work' as I truly love what I do.

And finally – to my family. Dad, thank you for a lifetime of support and for all the times you have readily played devil's advocate (sometimes you seem to enjoy playing this role a little too much!) Mum – thank you for all your love and care – I miss you. My sister Claire – you have been a role model and trailblazer for me in so many ways. My wonderful husband Matt who teaches me what unconditional love is, and Amelie, my new, precious daughter. This book is dedicated to you. Thank you for being the greatest gift of all.

About The Author

Prue Nichols has in-depth knowledge and experience of business and corporate practice, having spent six years working in International Public Relations. During this time she personally experienced all the typical work-related stress symptoms: from disrupted sleep patterns to digestive and hormonal problems. It was when she moved East to spend two years working in India and Thailand that, while immersed in a different culture, all the stress symptoms that Prue experienced regularly in London disappeared, without using conventional medical intervention.

Keen to understand how the body can heal itself naturally, Prue returned to the UK and spent four years studying how stress interplays between the mind and body. She founded The Orange Grove Natural Wellbeing in 2006, which focuses on alleviating stress by releasing physical and emotional tension. She also works with companies in the UK to reduce office stress and create energised, motivated employees.

For more information on The Energised Employee programme please email: prue@pruenichols.com

Praise of The Natural Laws of Work

"I highly recommend The Natural Laws of Work. It's really made me think long and hard about how I approach situations and offers some simple but extremely powerful solutions. From a company perspective it's also complimented our Health & Wellbeing Strategy beautifully!"
— Kelly Price – HR Manager: Computacenter UK

"Prue writes with diligence about the increasingly common problem of work stress, and provides really useful practical advice and exercises to help alleviate and manage stress in our everyday lives. A highly recommended and globally applicable read for individuals, HR professionals and strong people leaders."
— Hannah Larkin – Director: Global Talent Acquisition, Financial Services

"Prue provides great insight and understanding of stress management through practical applications: an excellent guide."
— Warren Hampton – General Manager: Operator and Broadcast Sector

"The wellbeing of our staff is a priority and ensuring that people are able to manage stress is an important aspect of that. This book addresses all facets of office life and is essential reading for anyone in business. I've bought copies for all of my employees."
— Tim Wayman – Managing Director: Robert Lee Distribution Ltd

"This is a great book that has the power to change your working life."
— James Town – Vice President: Financial Services Sector (EMEA)

"Working in the fast-paced, clinical and quite heartless world of investments banking, it is very easy to lose touch with oneself and the stress that is building up inside. Prue's book makes a very interesting and empowering read. It has enabled me to recognise the stress that I have just learnt to live with, the potential impact

of this stress and most importantly, effective ways in which to manage and control the symptoms and effects of this modern day condition to the benefit of my health and happiness."
— Richard Latimir – Vice President: Investment Banking

"Prue's approach to thriving in the workplace is simple yet powerful, and refreshingly real. I guarantee you'll feel the benefits of this down-to-earth and practical guide in all areas of life, not just the office."
— Katie Shellard – Founder: Urban Witch

"This book offers a fresh perspective on managing stress at work, with practical and rational suggestions on a subject matter that is both simple yet vast. I'm not sure I've ever seen a stress management book that weaves in lunar cycles and dry skin brushing so effortlessly! I will be recommending this book to all my clients."
— Avni Trivedi – Registered Osteopath

"This is a must read for anyone who works in an office, and brings the question of work-life balance to life. Prue's pratical examples can help anyone re-address their priorities in a realistic way."
— Lauren Kaye – Lawyer

"Prue's book is a must have for anyone who wants to take better care of themselves and lessen their stress levels. Her thorough research, engaging style and easy-to-follow tools help make easy, yet potentially life-transforming changes for all. Highly recommended: it is positive, informative and full of important facts for increasing our health and wellbeing."
— Claire Latimir – Founder: Holistic Heaven

"I thoroughly enjoyed The Natural Laws of Work. Prue combines clear, scientific facts in an easy to read, vibrant style. Clearly an expert in her field, Prue's book has significantly transformed my life inside and outside of the office. Everyone should read it."
— Jessica Spackman – Senior Consultant: Capgemini S.A

"Prue's book contains lots of great reminders and new ideas to maintain a healthy perspective on both work and play"
— Emma Flack – Global Communications Director FMCG

Introduction

To suggest that cultivating 'natural wellbeing' in the workplace is not only achievable but essential for optimal productivity can seem at odds with the demands of the today's corporate world where everything is focused on speed, competition and ambition. At a time of uncertainty, when the media constantly feeds us gloomy economic forecasts and visions of a shaky, unstable future, most of us believe that we should be grateful to have an income and a job at all. To expect to feel healthy, balanced and well during the hours of 9am to 5pm is deemed a luxury: something to aspire to once we have ticked-off everything else on the never-ending 'To-Do' list. As we battle to meet deadlines, placate clients and keep on top of our emails – personal wellbeing in the office gets relegated to the bottom of the list.

But is this really how it has to be? Is it sensible to prioritise economic survival over personal wellbeing? Might the cultivation of wellbeing lead to a better ability to juggle the demands of work, life and play? Perhaps we have been all too eager to pursue the former at the expense of the latter, only to find that if we get promoted to the job of our dreams, a lack of awareness regarding how to deal with the stress it will inevitably generate, makes the whole situation not only unhealthy, but unsustainable too.

Having experienced a great deal of stress in the workplace for many years I believe this to be so. We spend more time in the office than anywhere else so this is a good place to start our journey towards natural wellbeing and harmony. All too often we forego our own needs in the workplace with the misguided notion that work is the priority. However, unless we consider our health to be of upmost importance, then ultimately there will be a price to pay both mentally and physically.

The good news is that cultivating wellbeing in the workplace is not difficult, and with a little planning and focus is achievable by anyone.

Natural wellbeing is not complicated and it does not require us to turn our lives upside down. It's about understanding the core basics of who we are and how we work, and addressing a few of our lifestyle habits that are making us unhealthy.

Natural wellbeing at work is about having less stress, and more energy, vitality and joy in the place where we spend a great deal of our life.

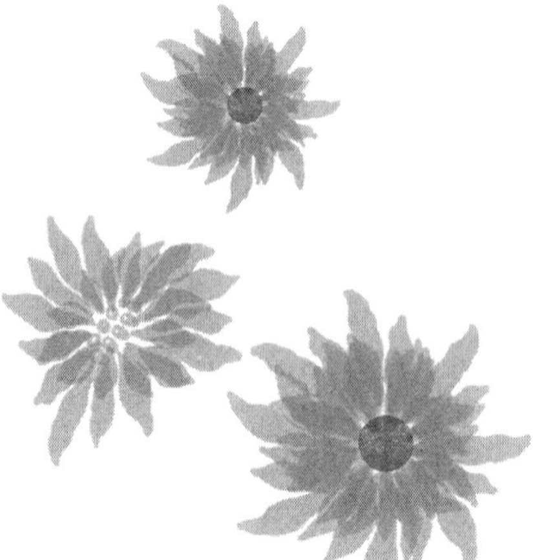

Contents

Natural Law No. 1
Responsibility 2

Natural Law No. 2
Water 16

Natural Law No. 3
Sugar 29

Natural Law No. 4
Movement 43

Natural Law No. 5
Tolerance 58

Natural Law No. 6
Beginning 73

Natural Law No. 7
Pause 85

Natural Law No. 8
Sleep 100

Natural Law No. 9
Nature 111

Natural Law No. 10
Passion 125

A Few Of My Favourite Things 137
Your Life of Wellbeing 141
Bibliography 142
Index 146

Natural Law No. 1

Responsibility

> *Stress is the twin sister of madness*
> — Chinese proverb

This first chapter is all about understanding the stress cycle and how stress can affect us in the workplace, because once we understand a few simple rules, then it is possible to have a completely different, less stressful experience at work. In order to really understand that WE control our stress levels, we need to understand what stress actually is and the impact it has on our mind and body. Whilst there is still no universally agreed definition of 'stress,' I think it is safe to say that most people have experienced varying levels of stress in their daily lives.

Now, just to be clear, I'm not talking about the type of stress that is 'buzzy'; that positive state of mind that makes us feel invincible. The technical word for that is *eustress* although I tend to call that welcome place excitement. No, the stress that I'm talking about here is the opposite kind; the overwhelming stress that changes our personality and outlook on life. I know only too well how I can be transported from being a rational, caring and compassionate human to quite the reverse, when I'm feeling stressed out. There is something about stress that can bring out the worst in us – and while we may try and suppress this change of character, there are times that we say and do things that we may later regret. For that reason alone, it is time to address the root causes of stress and learn how to alleviate them so that we do not become a victim of our own anxieties.

Responsibility

"When I'm stressed, the world becomes a different place. I stop thinking of people as people, but more like obstacles to be overcome. It feels like I'm solely responsible and I can't trust anyone to do anything right. My behaviour becomes much sharper and more snappy and while I can get away with this at work, I'm also more verbally attacking at home too. Unfortunately, my wonderful husband may even end up getting a torrent of abuse after making an innocent comment."

— Jessica, *Financial Analyst*

When I look back at my time working in Public Relations, there is one incident that stands out for me. Strangely nothing really dramatic happened and compared to other experiences that people endure throughout the world, my 'moment' would not have scored highly on a global stress scale. I wasn't made redundant, fired or forced to jump out of a burning office. I have no doubt that other people would have breezed through the circumstances without ruffling a feather. Indeed, I'm sure on another day I could have breezed through it without ruffling a feather myself, but the truth of the matter is that on that particular rainy November morning in 2001 I was lost in London, late for an appointment and very stressed in the back of a black taxi cab. My morning of difficulties culminated with me desperately (and I use that word advisedly) trying to find the CNBC studio so that I could brief my client. My client, an impatient man, had just called demanding to know where I was as he was due to go live on air on the 'Power Lunch' programme. My manager, an equally impatient and complex woman had also called demanding that I get to the studio immediately. Believe me, I wanted nothing more than to get the studio, but I just couldn't find the address, this being before the delights of Bluetooth. I was shaking and unable to think clearly as I tried to make sense of my A to Z map, hoping that if I stared long enough at the pages, the address would somehow materialise (it didn't). The driver – who I believe was also stressed – hurled abuse at me for not knowing where I was going and helped my stress level peak when he stopped the cab and ordered me to get out. I swore at him, he swore back and then drove off.

Now, if someone had told me (however kindly) at that moment that I was in control of my stress levels, I may very well be writing this from HMS Holloway prison, as right then it didn't feel like I was in control of anything. I could easily have vented my fury on any passer-by. It felt that everything – my client, my manager, the cab driver, the weather – was conspiring against me. Eventually, I found the studio and ever the professional, I duly put on my PR face and briefed my client before his appearance. I then raced dutifully back to the office to deal with the next item on my extensive 'To-Do' list. And whilst I was able to hold it together in the office (with the occasional silent snivel in the bathroom), when I got home, even with a large glass of Pinot Grigio, I continued to feel tense and anxious about what the next day would bring. Rarely in that job did I sleep well.

At this point in my early adult life, I didn't understand the human stress response, so while I may have often said silently or more often out loud, "God I'm stressed!" – I had very little understanding of what it actually meant when I uttered those words. And this so often seems to be the case with clients that I work with in the business world. In fact, for many people, they no longer recognise that they are experiencing stress symptoms as it is such a normal state of being for them, especially if other people around them are also displaying similar behaviour. Indeed, I used to think that anyone who was calm and laid back was either lazy or just didn't have enough work to do!

> "About six months into my first job, I went out for a meal with a university friend. After half an hour or so he said, 'You seem really different, I've never seen you so stressed - try and relax'. I remember feeling quite shocked by this – I didn't think I was stressed. It was only six months later when I spent a week working at a client's office that I realised how highly wired I was. I was so used to the being around forceful and stressed-out colleagues that I didn't realise there was another way to be."
> — Caroline, *Public Relations Officer*

In retrospect, I realise that if I'd had some understanding of how stress worked, my seven years in public relations would have been very different. Rather than feeling at the beck-and-call of others or a slave to my workload, I could have created more energy, vitality and most of all, more enjoyment in my job. This is a salutary lesson for us, as the CIPD (Chartered Institute of Personnel and Development) October 2011 survey showed: stress has become the most common cause of long-term sickness absence for both manual and non-manual employees. It also states that up to 80% of ill health can be traced to stress.

While I still do experience stress and have moments of 'behavioural regret', I don't react to stressful situations in the same way that I used to, mainly because I now understand the stress cycle. So without further ado, let's look at what happens when we 'get stressed'.

The Four Phases of the Stress Cycle: Trigger - Reaction - Release – Rest

We will be taking a closer look at actual stress triggers later in the book, but right now we're looking at what happens once we are triggered and in the stress response itself, which is also called the fight or flight response. This very fast hormonal reaction is outside of our mental control (part of the parasympathetic nervous system) and is a characteristic that we have inherited from our ancient ancestors. So while each of us has different stress triggers, once we're triggered we all physically respond in exactly the same way. Whilst it can feel very uncomfortable to be in a highly reactive fight or flight situation, it's actually a blessing that we have this in-built mechanism within our physiology. In fact it is very unlikely that we'd be still here, inhabiting planet earth if it were not for these 'sensory alarm bells', as it is the fight or flight response that made sure our ancestors got off their backsides when faced with a prehistoric predator.

To understand the stress response in action, let us imagine a prehistoric caveman outside of his cave, completely immersed in his work. Suddenly a sabre-toothed tiger comes into view: immediately and totally subconsciously, alarm bells trigger our caveman's focus from work to survival. Within seconds stress hormones including adrenaline, cortisol and DHEA flood his bloodstream, making his whole body pumped-up and surging with energy. His heart rate, blood rate and oxygen flow all dramatically increase while his digestive system and sex drive shut down. All physical activity is focused purely on survival and ensuring that our caveman is ready for action.

The caveman will physically respond either by facing his predator head on (fight) or running for the hills (flight). Once the danger has passed and if the caveman lived to tell the tale, he would then rest for a short amount of time to allow his hormone levels to return to normal before carrying on with the rest of his day, physically pretty much unaffected by his sabre-toothed tiger encounter. From these kinds of scenario, cave-dwellers evolved and learned how to protect themselves from such threats.

This centuries-old cycle is still the same today, the only trouble is that nowadays we don't follow the cycle through to its natural conclusion. As our work means that we are usually confined to an office, car or meeting room, it's easy for us to get stuck in the second stage - the hormonal reaction. Without having an outlet for physical release, all that pent-up stress-induced adrenaline swirls around our blood stream for up to six hours creating tightness, tension and a general feeling of being ill-at-ease. While I certainly don't encourage road rage or other acts of physical violence to get rid of the adrenaline, these urges are actually our body's natural response to stress. Therefore, it is imperative that we find new ways to release the adrenaline and allow our body to relax and regain its natural balance.

However, even if we do manage to reach stage three and create an outlet for physical release, many of us forego the last stage - rest. I'm not talking about taking a week-long break after doing a stressful fifteen-minute presentation to one's colleagues, I'm talking about ensuring that we create some 'time-out' in our day whether it is ten minutes to recharge our batteries by a walk in the park or a soothing massage after work. Too often we jump from one stress trigger to another without taking time to breathe properly let alone stop and rest – and then we wonder why at the end of the day we feel either wired or completely wiped out.

Rest is such a critical part of the stress cycle as it enables our body to rebalance its endocrine system - the system responsible for sending out all stress-related hormones such as adrenaline, cortisol and DHEA. If our adrenal glands are not given time to recuperate after a stressful situation, they will become out of balance. Too much adrenaline leaves us in a restless state, unable to relax or switch-off our racing minds and we can also experience physical symptoms such as excessive sweating – especially at night – and disrupted digestive and sleep patterns. Ultimately this can lead to adrenal burn-out which is a state of total exhaustion, the remedy for which bed rest for extended periods of time. It makes sense then to rest, relax and recuperate before such a regimen is forced upon us.

"Like most people, I had a really busy and demanding life. Although the nature of my job was full-on and the pace was relentless, I didn't have the time to stop even though I started to notice that my energy and concentration levels were noticeably dwindling. Mornings became especially hard as I was unable to get any proper, good quality sleep. Normal every day activities got harder as I tried to carry on and ignore the overwhelming feeling of exhaustion. After six months it got to the point when I was unable to get out of bed and had to have three months off work. This was one of the hardest and most frustrating times of my life. I'd say that it's taken me two years to recover and fully feel like myself again."
— Jonathan, *Estate Agent*

Throughout the 'developed' world, there seems to be a mindset amongst business-people that 'doing nothing' is a sign of laziness. Epithets such as 'Time is Money' and 'Sleep is for Wimps' mean that relaxing and resting is frowned upon. Yet rest is a gentle, natural healing process that can boost our wellbeing fundamentally. The easiest and most effective thing that any of us can do to support natural wellbeing is to give ourselves time to rest deeply. We all want to do the best we can and often push ourselves when actually what we really need to work effectively is to take time to stop, relax and recharge our inner batteries. We're not like the pink Duracell rabbit that can just keep on going, and it's not natural for us to do that anyway. So while we may believe that we're indispensable and are too busy to take those precious moments to rest, in the long run we pay a high price for ignoring the last stage of the stress cycle as our bodies will eventually go on strike, resulting in a much longer, enforced stop.

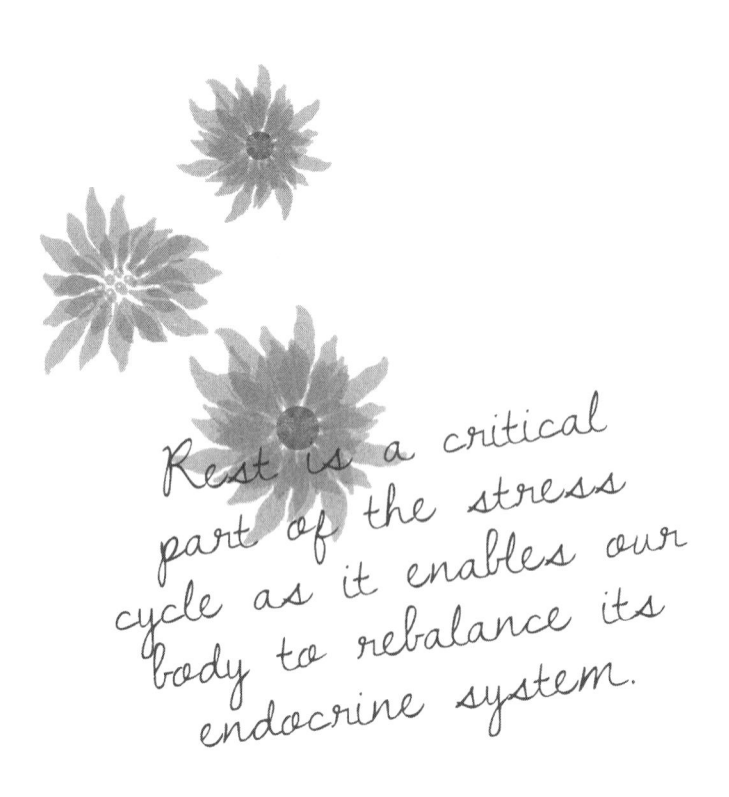

Rest is a critical part of the stress cycle as it enables our body to rebalance its endocrine system.

Our Reptilian Shadow

There is another part of the stress response that is also important to be aware of – the personality change that occurs. If you take a moment to reflect back to the last time you were in the stress response, try and remember how you behaved towards other people, whether it be angry thoughts that you internalised, or even said out loud; or kicking a chair or slamming a door... We all do it: our normally rational behaviour momentarily evaporates and is replaced by temperamental aggressiveness. I still cringe on remembering being late for a meeting in London. Time-keeping, or more specifically being late, is one of my personal stress triggers, so in this particular case, every rational thought had disappeared from my head as I ran to the meeting muttering blasphemies at young children taking up space on the pavement; I caused an old man to stumble and shouted at a car that did not let me cross the road. So what is about stress that changes my usually caring self to some alien creature who does not care or consider her fellow human beings?

Well, while I am not making excuses for my behaviour there is a reason for this. When we're in fight or flight mode, blood is diverted from the frontal cortex of our brains and re-routed to the hindbrain, which has several repercussions for us: the frontal cortex is concerned with more humanitarian issues such as reasoning, empathy and compassion. Now in a fight/flight or life/death situations, these qualities aren't necessarily a priority. So it makes sense that the blood is sent away from the front part of our brain, which could potentially hinder our survival and sent to the hindbrain.

Now, the hindbrain is a piece of anatomy that we actually share with reptiles: this part of the brain positively thrives on dominance, power and aggression as these are the exact qualities that we need to get us out of danger – well certainly in the past, when the dangers tended to be more physical. In the boxing match where Mike Tyson infamously bit off Evander Holyfield's ear, this kind of instinctive aggression is a good (if not gory) example of the hindbrain in action.

This helps to explain why, when we are stressed, we behave differently and act in an animalistic way. It can also help us to understand why our colleagues can say and do irrational things when under pressure. Rather than take it personally, it is so much more beneficial to have compassion for ourselves and our colleagues, and see that we all are, whether we realise it or not, in fight or flight mode – in the throes of an ancient evolutionary survival mechanism that operates from our 'reptilian personality'.

Side-effects of the Stress Response

At this point we need to ask, does it matter? Is there a problem with yo-yoing in and out of the stress response? After all, no one is nice all the time and surely this keeps us alert and on our toes, especially in the office, where (let's be honest), the sabre-toothed tiger has been replaced by a different type of predator!

Well yes, it does matter for a number of reasons. The stress response evolved as a survival mechanism for extreme circumstances, but the pressures of modern living mean that it is almost permanently switched-on. When we're exhausting our hard-working adrenaline glands and living constantly in fight or flight mode, this hugely impacts our health and wellbeing. Also, because we stay in stage two (the hormonal reaction) for longer periods of time, this depletes our reserves and immune system so that we inevitably have less energy, vitality and motivation. And this isn't just contained in the workplace: our physical and mental state spills over into our evenings and weekends.

"Although the sector that I work in is renown for being incredibly stressful, when I first started work, I relished each project as I really believed that I could make a difference. However, 10 stressful years later, I feel exhausted and ground down. Issues and problems that once fuelled me now overwhelm me and I feel constantly anxious. Rather than being able to leave my work in the office, I find myself worrying about my job at home, which makes me impatient and short with my husband and children. I often wake up in the middle of the night thinking about work problems as I can't seem to get my mind to switch off. My whole body feels tight and the tension in my neck and shoulders gives me headaches and a general feeling of heaviness and discomfort."

— Lucy, *Care Co-ordinator*

There May Be Trouble Ahead

In the national media, it seems we are bombarded almost daily by the latest scientific reports that link stress to a whole host of diseases: from irritable bowel syndrome to high blood pressure and heart attacks. The BBC Radio 4's documentary 'Stressed Out' broadcast in 2000 stated that a person in Britain dies every three to four minutes from a heat attack, which they said is often directly related to stress. Whilst it is undoubtedly true that stress has major health implications for the body, rather than focus on all the different stress related diseases that can occur, I feel it is more important to understand how we can manage the root causes of these illnesses to try and prevent them in the first place.

To understand this we need to step back and gain a bigger perspective of how our bodies work. We can only ever be in two states:

1. Fight or Flight
2. Rest and Repair

These states are also referred to as the sympathetic and parasympathetic systems, which we'll talk about more in Chapter 7. As we know, when we're in fight or flight mode, we're in a state of defence/attack – while this important in our long term survival, it's actually pretty exhausting as we're constantly on edge, waiting for the onslaught.

The second stage – rest and repair – is where our body does all it's core maintenance work, repairing cells, detoxifying blood, ensuring that our bodies can maintain natural homeostasis (balance) and wellbeing. This vital work is often done when we're relaxing or asleep. It's impossible for our bodies to be in fight or flight and rest and repair at the same time.

So, if we're spending longer in fight or flight mode than rest or repair, it means that our bodies are unable to carry out vital maintenance work, which stops us from functioning at our optimum level and our natural wellbeing will be eroded. These signs are often very gradual and it can take many forms: from frequently picking up colds, coughs or flu and having trouble getting rid of them, to feeling exhausted even when you wake up – or just some inner sense that things aren't quite right and that you're not functioning at 100%. Any upset to your digestive system or noticeable change to your sex drive is also a clue, as during fight or flight our digestive system and sex drive shuts down as blood is sent to extremities and muscles. These are just some of the signs that we're spending too long in the stress cycle.

Just How Stressed Are We?

Although there are stress tests that we can take, I don't advocate a 'one-size-fits-all' approach, as we all deal with stress differently depending on what is going on in our lives. Some of my clients would not even consider that they are stressed, however on gentle investigation of their physical state, it becomes clear to them that there are signals that stress is building up.

We're all different and will have different stress tolerances – sometimes we can cope with many triggers at once, and other times, it can be something very small such as someone snoring opposite us on the train, that can send us into the stress response. The most important thing is that we listen to our bodies and notice our own reactions. The list below highlights certain symptoms that are representative of stress being present:

Mental stress symptoms

- Tiredness
- Difficulty sleeping – either getting to sleep or staying asleep
- Irritability
- Lack of vitality

Physical stress symptoms

- Tiredness
- Headaches
- Tightness in muscles - especially shoulders and neck
- Irritable bowel syndrome
- Any digestive problems
- Excessive sweating
- Shallow breathing

The workplace is where we are likely to experience our highest levels of stress, if we are not proactive in managing our stress levels. The somewhat artificial environment at work – where we have to spend long hours with people we don't necessarily like, in a space that is often poorly designed and ventilated – can be a stress hub. It is not surprising therefore, that according to the Work Foundation's 'Stress at Work' report, work-related stress results in the loss of nearly 13 million working days each year. Research by Professor Tarani Chandola for the British Academy shows that women are more likely to have higher stress levels than men as they often take on responsibility for managing home life too. Many women actually start their working day highly stressed, dogged by the feeling that there is too much to do and too little time to do it.

Dealing With Stress – a pill for every ill?

Allopathic or 'mainstream' medicine focuses on suppressing stress symptoms. So whilst a painkiller gets rid of a headache, what is of utmost consideration is that the headache is telling us that something is not quite right. So, rather than blocking-out pain or discomfort, we would be so much better off taking some time to listen to our bodies to find out what we need to do to alleviate the specific symptoms. This can be unnerving and it requires courage to trust ourselves, but the current quick-fix mentality is doing a disservice to our bodies, which work so hard for us.

> "Before I left my marketing job in London, days were long and stress levels were high, although at the time, I didn't realise how stressed I was, because it was my normal state of being. My digestive system was slow, I had tingling sensations in my hands and I often felt like I couldn't take enough breath. Combined with late nights of drinking, my immune system wasn't very happy and I'd often come down with colds and flu, but I didn't want to take time off work for fear of projects and campaigns falling behind. I self-medicated with Nurofen to block out my sore throats, headaches and feeling of being 'run down'. This only worked temporarily and enabled me to get through the day (taking a higher dose than recommended!) but eventually my body started shouting louder and I'd be forced to bed with a fever... and ultimately had to take more time off work than I would've done if I'd just rested for a day and looked after myself with nutritious food and natural remedies. Now when I start to feel run down, I make time to rest and listen to my body, because no job (no matter how important) takes priority over my health."
>
> — Katie, *Copywriter*

Each chapter of this book will share a secret for natural wellbeing so that by the end of this book, you'll not only understand your own reaction to stress but have a raft of techniques to lower your stress levels and rebalance naturally. When we take responsibility for our own wellbeing rather than avoiding and shutting off from what our bodies are trying to tell us, then we really will thrive inside and outside the workplace.

Visualisation Exercise

- Close your eyes and take three deep breaths:

- See yourself in the office at your most stressed. How does it feel in your body? Where are you noticing tension being held? How are people reacting to you? What word describes how you are feeling?

- Now imagine yourself in the office feeling cool, calm and collected. How does that feel in your body? How are other people reacting to you? What word describes how you are feeling?

- Write the first words that come to mind for each exercise on a Post-It note and keep it in on your desk. When you notice your stress levels rising, use these words as a reminder of the two different ways that you can be in the office.

Natural Law No. 2

Water

> "You are not sick, you are thirsty."
> — Dr F Batmanghelidj *Your Body's Many Cries for Water*

Before we start, I think it's important we acknowledge that when we're racing round the office in 'headless chicken' mode, that the actual *cause* of our stress isn't necessarily what we think it is. For example, I always used to think that my stress was being caused by something or someone; ranging from a difficult client – I had one in particular and just seeing her number flash on my phone would make my stomach churn – or a looming deadline or that 'complex' manager I've briefly made reference to in the past. I used to believe that if the situation was different or the person was dead (or more charitably, on holiday!) then my life would be easier and certainly much less stressful. Yet while colleagues can increase our stress levels – and we'll discuss this more in chapter 5 – in actual fact colleagues are a minor stress trigger when compared to a lack of water, because, let me to blunt – if we're not drinking enough water we will be totally stressed out. This simple natural law is a revelation to most people.

When we're dehydrated (ie: our body requires more water than we're giving it), we unconsciously enter that ancient, inbuilt hormonal stress response that we refer to as the fight or flight mode. While there are a few of us in the developed world, who *are* actually drinking enough water, the majority of us live our lives on planet earth not so much as 'the living dead' but one step removed: the living dehydrated. Think how compromised one's health must be living in drought-prone countries and how important the work of charities such as Water Aid is in addressing this fundamental bodily need.

Now, you may fit into one of two camps (or, perhaps like I used to, you yo-yo between them both): either you think water is important or you don't think water is important. For years I slid between both camps – I had a vague awareness that water was important but this did not necessarily translate into drinking much of it. It was a bit like knowing that salt was bad for me but not being able to tell you why. I knew on some level that water was important but was so confused by all the contradictory information out there that I was never sure what to believe. There's much contradictory advice about water: that it is dangerous to drink too much of it, and conversely that you can never drink too much water. Knowing what to do can feel like a minefield, but the key is to tune-in to your body's needs. What is your body saying to you about its need for water? Once we understand why our bodies need water, it's much, much easier to make an informed decision about drinking it.

The Basic Facts

Like the earth, which is 70% water, when we are in a state of healthy balance, we too are approximately 70% water. After oxygen, water is the most important substance that our bodies require – we couldn't live for much more than 10 days without it. Our wonderful, magnificent bodies are a combination of over a 100 trillion cells and each cell is 70% water except for cells in the brain which are 85% water. We are the result of the combined interactions of all of our cells and what is happening in one cell is a reflection of what is happening throughout our body. The health of each little cell directly corresponds to our overall health and indeed, our happiness. This is a rather wordy way of saying, "We are our cells". Ideally, we want our cells to be as healthy as possible and luckily, our cells are pretty low-maintenance and work incredibility hard under some frankly downright shocking conditions we subject them to. But there is one thing that they need: water. We can keep our cells (and therefore ourselves) happy, quite simply by drinking plenty of fresh, pure water.

> "The average body is 70 per cent water. We start out life being 99 percent water as fetuses. When we are born, we are 90 per cent water and by the time we reach adulthood we are down to 70 per cent water. If we die of old age, we will probably be about 50 per cent water. In other words, throughout our lives we exist mostly as water. When I realised this and started to look at the world from this perspective, I began to see things in a whole new way."
> — Masaru Emoto, *The Hidden Messages in Water*

Each cell, depending on where they are positioned in the body, has a very important job to do. We are not aware of what each cell is doing on a moment to moment basis, but their combined effort ensures that we can live, breathe, ingest, digest and excrete – and function as a rational human being (well, most of the time anyway!). As the cell's work can only take place in water, any decrease in the amount of water has a BIG impact on the productivity of the cell. So when sources start to dwindle, the cell cannot do its job properly. A message is sent to the brain that this is a life and death situation and the body enters into fight or flight mode. Imagine being in a desert with the sun beating down on you and there is no oasis in sight. Well that's a metaphor for how a cell reacts when it doesn't have enough water. Any water reserves (often found in the brain or colon) are re-routed by the pituitary gland and sent to the highest priority functions: anything that isn't life critical (like sex drive) gets put on hold.

During such times of 'drought', any water that is in the body is held onto tightly. So, often when we have swollen ankles or water retention, the message that the body is trying to tell us is that it's holding onto water for dear life, as it doesn't know where the next drop is coming from. Sadly, and completely understandably, many people when they suffer from water retention stop drinking under the false belief that there is too much water in the body.

So, apart from a delay in important health maintenance, swollen body parts and being in a constant state of fight or flight, lack of water means that rather than having a flexible, fluid, water-based environment, our stressed cell becomes shrivelled and a shadow of its former self. Rather than having a healthy liquid environment to communicate with other cells, it becomes rigid and hard and some less important cells will die off. Now, while we won't completely shrivel on the outside, we'll feel this change in our cell's environment, because when our cells become rigid, so do we, both mentally and physically.

Having studied the body's need for water for years now, I notice very quickly when I've become dehydrated as my thought processes are affected: I lose creativity, become quite narrow-minded and am much less clear and rational in how I express myself. Whenever I hear anyone say that they feel 'tight' or 'alone' or 'cut-off' then I immediately link this to what is happening in their cells as these statements are classic dehydration messages.

Many years ago when I was waiting to fly home from an oversees work trip, a message on the airport 'Departures' board flashed up to say that the flight was going to be delayed by ten hours. Once the initial shock and annoyance dissipated, I settled down to read my book and while-away the hours. After a few hours, I noticed how anxious and panicky I was feeling. It felt very different to the annoyance that I experienced earlier, and I was really worried and restless combined with feeling totally alone, trapped in the airport. I remembered, after ten long minutes of indulging in these feelings (wondering if it was subliminal message from my subconscious not to get on the flight!) that I had not drunk anything since I arrived.

I bought a bottle of water and after drinking it, within minutes felt totally different. Honestly, the change in my mental attitude was that quick! Yes, I still had a long tedious wait ahead of me but I felt 100% calmer and had clarity and perspective once more. The incredible thing was the *rate* at which drinking water transformed my stress levels. Reflecting back on my PR days, I rarely drank water at all – on some days my only water consumption was when I cleaned my teeth! I now believe that so much of my stress at that time was due to the fact that I (my cells, me) were desperately lacking water.

> "I never used to think of water until I attended the Energised Employee course. Everything that Prue said about water made complete sense – I had just never considered that my ability to do my job was influenced by how much water I drank. It was funny that after that session, the next week we all turned up for the course with water bottles. Now, as soon as I feel stressed, I immediately drink a glass of water – I feel instantly better, more awake and in control."
> — Marion, *Business Analyst*

Dr B

At this point it seems relevant to introduce you to Dr Fereydoon Batmanghelidj. Dr B as I shall call him, was an internationally renowned researcher who studied under the Nobel Prize winner Sir Alexander Fleming. He spent his years training in London at St Mary's Hospital and was in his home country of Iran doing medical research when the Iranian Revolution broke out in 1979. Being in the wrong place at the wrong time, he ended up spending two years in Evin prison – a pretty tough hell-hole.

However, it was during his imprisonment that his medical mission completely changed, as one night, Dr B had to treat a fellow prisoner with crippling peptic ulcer pain. With no medication available, Dr B gave him two glasses of water and hoped for the best. Within eight minutes, his patient's pain disappeared. He instructed the prisoner to drink two glasses of water every three hours and he became pain free for his four remaining months in prison. Wondering if this was a one-off, Dr B went on to successfully treat 3000 fellow prisoners suffering from stress-induced diseases with water. He used the rest of his time in prison (even refusing an early release option) to study how water could heal other diseases and stress-induced problems. In all cases, Dr B found that water alone, cured these imbalances and in his book *Your Body's Many Cries for Water* his message was clear: that *all* disease, physical imbalance and stress is due to dehydration.

"During nearly three years of my captivity, I cured over 3,000 ulcer cases with only water in Tehran's Evin Prison - my 'God-given stress laboratory'. All thanks to water: plain, simple, cost-free medicine for everyone. Water that we all take for granted! Water that the medical profession has dismissed as unworthy of research! Since my eyes were opened to water as a natural medication, I have developed and applied this technique to the point where it has alleviated and healed hundreds of traditionally incurable sicknesses and chronic pains."

— Dr Batmanghelidj, *Your Body's Many Cries for Water*

So, while we're lucky that there are many options available to us if we are in pain, the simple and cheapest option is often overlooked. Water.

How Much Is Enough?

So now we understand why water is important, the next question is how much should we be drinking? Well, whilst we are all different, and as such need differing amounts depending on whether we are sitting at a desk all day or running across London to various meetings, the general rule of thumb is two litres of water per day. This tends to have one of two reactions with my clients: first reaction is a sharp intake of breath, followed by, "I can't possibly drink that much!" The second reaction is much more *laissez faire:* "Oh is that all?"

While two litres of water per day may sound like a lot, especially if we're used to taking just a few sips every now and then, the reason why this is often given as a daily recommendation is because this is the amount required for us to 'break even'. We need two litres to replace water lost though talking, sweating, digesting, excreting and breathing as well as when at work, coping with the dehydrating effects of the office heating and air-conditioning.

Depending where you are on the water-intake scale, please don't think that you need to achieve this daily goal of two-litres overnight: work up to this amount slowly. In the first few weeks, you may need to go to the toilet more but this should not be a reason to avoid drinking in the first place. Imagine pouring water over a parched hanging basket: a lot of if will drain away, but even in that hardened, dry state, some water will be retained. This is what happens to our cell when we start drinking after being in that desertified state. It takes time for optimum levels of water to be absorbed back into our cells, but eventually it will make a difference, and remember why you are drinking more – to lower those stress levels!

I remember a few years ago talking to an older client about water and she said that she did not buy into the theory as her parents did not drink water and they lived to a ripe old age. She was convinced it's all a con. And while my grandparents (or parents for that matter) did not walk around with water bottles either, it's true to say that the world has changed dramatically in the last thirty years. Never have we crammed more into twenty-four hours: balancing work, children, family and friends. There are many, many more chemicals in our environment, which means that we require more water to flush out the toxins inside and outside of our bodies.

I believe our bodies need more water than ever to cope with the work/life balance – whether we realise it or not. And often it's easy to overlook the signals that our cells send us requesting water. Often we misread our cell's messages for water by providing ourselves with a 'solution' that dehydrates us even more such as drinking coffee or alcohol. So many liquids such as fizzy drinks, juices and teas available in the supermarkets will exasperate the problem as they are filled with ingredients that turn off our natural thirst mechanism so we don't realize we're thirsty. They also require the body to use large amounts of water to dilute and flush these out of the body. Remember our cells are 70% water not 70% Red Bull!

> "In medical school, we learned that a dry mouth is a reliable sign of dehydration. But it is not the only one. It is very common for a child (or adult) to feel hungry when in fact she is thirsty. The body

also get 'thirst pains', the same way it gets hunger pains, so another sign of dehydration is actual aches and pains. Though the body can survive some dehydration it eventually pays a price. In adults, chronic dehydration can lead to conditions such as dyspepsia (heartburn), arthritic pain, back pain, headache (including migraine), colitis pain and associated constipation, angina pain (from the heart) and leg pain (on walking). This is in addition to the common symptom of fatigue, particularly mid-afternoon".

— Dr Christiane Northrup, *Mother-Daughter Wisdom*

To help us understand our body's cries for water, I have outlined the five classic messages that our body sends us (or shows to us) when it wants a tall, fresh glass of H2O.

The Five Classic Cries For Water

1. *I've got a headache!*

This is the most common cry that our cells send forth, and really it's no wonder that we get a headache and find it hard to concentrate when those cells which need more water than the rest of our body, are gasping up there in the brain. Although no one can as yet explain why the headache occurs, some experts believe that when there is not enough water in the brain, the blood vessels narrow, which reduces the amount of water and oxygen able to reach to brain, resulting in a headache. Whatever the reason, whenever you notice a headache, reach for a (large) glass of the water and notice the difference between that and an aspirin.

2. *I'm hungry!*

Misreading the thirst signal and thinking that it's a sign that we need to eat is also very common. If you ever feel that you could eat and eat and eat then it's a sure sign that you're mistaking that hunger feeling and need to drink instead. Until you drink some water, you'll keep feeling hungry and if you (like me) have limited willpower then you'll be over-feeding your dehydrated cells. This will make you more dehydrated as the cells have to find water from somewhere to dilute all the excess food. Consequently, we can just see those stress levels rise. To be on the safe side, have a glass of water when you notice you're hungry. Either this will satiate your thirst desire or you were actually hungry and thus if you give it 20 minutes you will have prepared your stomach and intestines for ultimate digestion. Of course, if you do notice that you feel thirsty then this is a sure sign that your body is very dehydrated so drink some water – now.

3. *My urine is dark!*

Okay, so this one is not actually a cry, but more of a sign. Urine is a great indicator of how hydrated or dehydrated we are. Made in the kidneys, urine is the watery substance that your body uses to get rid of any excess chemicals and minerals. Ideally urine should be a light straw colour (as this shows it has travelled through the kidneys) – if it's clear, it generally means that your body can't hold on to water (think of the hanging plant analogy) as it is passing straight through. Increasing good quality Omega 3 into your diet such as krill oil, can help with this. If your urine is dark, this is a sign that you are dehydrated and need to drink more water. But, I'll make an exception here: you can drink some of your own urine instead of water if you must! I know this sounds a little strange but actually, urine therapy has been used for centuries as the best natural healer that you can find. The book *Your Own Perfect Medicine* is a great guide for those interested in learning more about this.

4. *I'm constipated!*

Constipation is a common sign that we are not drinking enough water, as the body doesn't want to waste any water being flushed out with the stools. Instead, water that has been stored in the colon to help stools pass out easily and comfortably is sent back for another tour of duty. This means that our stools are harder and likely to cause irritation and discomfort on evacuation, and the liver and kidneys have to work harder as they need to clean the colon water before it can be used again. Drinking a glass of water is much, much less hassle, I promise you!

5. *My back hurts!*

If you haven't had a back injury or regularly experience problems in this area from a known cause, then back pain can also be a cry for water. The pain/ache/discomfort is felt in the lower (lumbar) part of the back where your kidneys live – just under where the bra straps sits – although pain can be felt a bit lower too. The kidneys dilute toxins in the body, so when there is not enough water to dilute or flush them out, toxins build up. Dr Christiane Northrup, the world's leading authority in the field of women's health and wellbeing adds that many aches and pains are in fact 'thirst pains'. This follows the research of Dr B who says that all pain is an indicator of dehydration as the lack of water means that sensory nerve endings are not working properly.

It's best to be on the safe side and drink water regularly!

Too Much of a Good Thing?

So what happens if we honor every cry or twinge from our body with water? Can we have too much of a good thing? Well, like most things we need to drink water in moderation as excessive water consumption (5 litres plus) dilutes sodium levels in our blood and can lead to a condition called 'water intoxication'. This is a condition in which electrolyte imbalance and tissue swelling affects the brain. While there are cases of people who have died from drinking too much water, these instances are very rare and there is often an underlying medical problem that overrides our natural desire to stop. If we are healthy and in a rational state of mind, then we're unlikely to drink too much. However, if you notice that you're drinking a lot of water (2-3 litres plus) and still feeling thirsty, then it's best to pop along to your local GP as this can been a signal that your body is out of balance and something needs addressing. However as long as you follow the two-litres rule and spread this out throughout the day then you'll be fine.

What Type of Water?

This is a tricky one and the best I can offer is an overview for if we lived in an ideal world. Some water is better than no water but there are other things that we should be aware of, as not all water is equal. Firstly the water should be body temperature: if it's too cold, the water has to be held in the stomach and warmed up; if it's too hot then again it is held in the stomach until it is cooled down. Body temperature (37°C) is ideal as our cells can immediately absorb it.

Now, regardless of what water companies tell us, tap water is full of chemicals and by drinking it we're absorbing the less desirable constituents too. There are lots of different filters available: from appliances that you connect to your taps, to a standard water jug filter and it is well worth investing in the best filtration system you can afford. It is important to be aware of the different descriptions on water bottles. There are three types to choose from 'mineral' water, 'spring' water and 'other' which is often described as table water. Mineral water is without doubt the best type of water as it has been filtered by the mountains and is bottled at source. However, while' spring' water is also bottled at source, it is treated with less natural substances to improve its purity. 'Other' can come from anywhere including your tap!

Bottled water is also a controversial option as chemicals from the plastic can leech into the bottle – so they shouldn't be placed in the sun or reused. Glass bottles are the best, although they are heavy and lugging one around definitely can be a workout.

So, have a think about what works best for you. The Dr Mercola website has an excellent article looking at all the different water options. While it is aimed at an American audience, it is useful reading if you want to have a good overview of all your different options: www.mercola.com

Why Tea and Coffee Doesn't Count

Sorry to give you the bad news but actually tea and coffee (especially coffee) will actually make you more dehydrated and thus, more stressed. The reason why is that they are both 'diuretics', which means that they make you pee more and force good water out too. However, rather than feel deprived, the best thing to do when you want to enjoy tea or coffee, is to drink a glass of water first, this way you'll be replacing any lost fluid and you won't be expecting the drink to alleviate your thirst.

I Hate Water!

It's hard to actually hate water as it's inoffensive and doesn't really taste of much. However there are people that think it's boring. Well it really doesn't have to be: while I'm not talking about adding orange or lemon squash to jazz it up (this creates work for the body as it needs to dilute the concentrate), there are other flavours that we can include. Adding a slice of lemon or lime is excellent as this will actually make the drink more alkaline and more hydrating. Also adding mint or fresh herbs to the water can also make it taste more refreshing and interesting.

Just a Perfect Day

Once I realised that I was dehydrated I had a beautiful jug that sat on my office desk - it held two litres and I knew that by the end of the day, I needed to have it finished. Now, as I'm less likely to be at a desk all day, I just break the amount down into 4 pints. I have a pint 20 minutes before I eat as this allows for optimum digestion. Ideally we shouldn't drink lots of water whilst we're eating as this upsets the pH balance required for digestion.

Visulisation Exercise

- Close your eyes and take three deep breaths:

- Imagine one of the cells in your body. What does it looks like? How much water does it contain? Does it have a message for you?

- Now imagine that cell filled with pure, fresh water. What does it look like now? How does it feel? What does your cell want to tell you?

- Write down the message that you receive in a place that you look at regularly such as your diary.

Natural Law No. 3

Sugar

"It would be extraordinary if sugar, known to wreak havoc on the teeth, did not also have profound repercussions elsewhere in the body."
— William Duffy *Sugar Blues*

If we don't want to be stressed-out, then we need to avoid sugar, as contrary to popular advertising, sugar does not make us feel better. It seems unfair really as most of us have a tendency to like sweet things. It feels comforting and a real treat to have a bar of chocolate at the end of a long day, or a donut with a cup of coffee (two stress-inducing habits in one!) While Sticky toffee pudding is one of the UK's favourite deserts, a trip to the cinema would not be the same without a massive bucket of sugary popcorn. Naturally occurring sweet foods, such as fruits, are good to eat in moderation, but highly-processed, sugar-laden sweets are actually harmful to the body and should be limited or preferably, avoided.

"In the summer of 1965, I met a wise man from the East, a Japanese philosopher who had just returned from several weeks in Saigon. 'If you really expect to conquer the North Vietnamese,' he told me 'you must drop Army PXs on them – sugar, candy and Coca-Cola. That will destroy them faster than bombs.'"
— William Duffy, *Sugar Blues*

The raw, natural form of sugar is found in sugar cane. As this incorporates many additional vitamins and minerals, it provides us with a good, balanced source of energy. The trouble is this natural food source has been corrupted as we have extracted the sweetness from the cane through a refining process. While this does make products masquerading as food taste 'better', the lack of nutrients means that there is no nutritional buffer so the sugar enters our blood stream very quickly. This causes all sorts of physical and emotional health problems and before we know it, we're hooked into an addictive and destructive blood sugar rollercoaster.

> "I have no desire to pussyfoot around this one. White refined sugar is without question more dangerous to our health than any other food product. Sugar is not only becoming the new tobacco in terms of addiction, but it now contributes to more degenerative disease and premature deaths than tobacco."
> — Jason Vale, *Turbo Charge Your Life in 14 Days*

Blood Sugar – the key to sanity

The refined white or brown granules that we have in our cupboards may be labelled as sugar, but they are actually far-removed from their natural state and have no nutritional value to us. This 'sugar impostor' is in fact alien to nature and also affects us in ways that are unnatural as well. For us to understand this, we need to have a simple overview of how our blood sugar levels work, as this is critical if we want to be mentally balanced and stress-free in the office. There are two types of hormones involved in maintaining our blood sugar levels: insulin, which lowers blood sugar by storing it in the cells; and glucogen which increases blood sugar by converting stored fat into sugar. While the process is actually very simple, it does involve some terminology that relates back to school biology lessons, so just in case, like me, your brain is a little rusty, I've included a reminder below:

Glucose: Produced when we eat carbohydrates. This is the main source of energy for our cells as well as the main type of sugar found in our blood.

Glycogen: Needed to maintain homeostasis. Excess glucose in the blood is converted into glycogen, which is then stored in the muscles and liver.

Homeostasis: Vital internal processes that make sure we remain in balance and can continue to live.

High blood sugar: Too much glucose in the blood - we feel energised, wired, restless.

Low blood sugar: Not enough glucose in the blood - we will feel stressed, irritable, unable to concentrate. This is usually followed by a sugar craving, and if fulfilled, will swing us into high blood sugar mode.

How Blood Sugar Works

After we have eaten a meal, carbohydrates are broken down into glucose (energy) which is absorbed through the wall of the intestine and enters the blood stream. In order for our cells to use this glucose for energy, the pancreas produces insulin that acts as a 'key' allowing the glucose to enter the cell.

As the acid/alkaline balance of our blood has to be carefully maintained and can't metabolise more than a teaspoon of glucose at any time, excess glucose is converted into glycogen and stored in the liver and muscles. As the liver's capacity is limited, large doses of glycogen cause our liver to expand like a big balloon. Now (and I find this part fascinating), when the liver reaches its maximum capacity – imagine a balloon just amount to pop – the excess glycogen is returned to the blood in the form of fatty acids.

To protect our vital organs, these fatty acids, rather like unwanted guests, are distributed throughout the body and stored in our most inactive areas: stomach, buttocks, breasts and thighs. Once these get filled, the fatty acids are then distributed around our active organs such as the heart and kidneys causing all manner of undesirable consequences. Not ideal.

To avoid this, we need to eat slow-releasing carbohydrates that enter our blood stream slowly. When we eat refined sugars (the 'empty' sugars that have been stripped of vitamins and minerals) our blood sugar dramatically spikes as it is broken down into glucose very quickly. While this does give us a sudden rush of energy, it also means that just as quickly as it has risen, it will also drop leaving us in an undesirable place called low blood sugar. As well as giving us a false hit of energy, foods containing refined sugars will also leave us hungry as this empty sugar, devoid of nutrients will not fill us up. Consequently we tend to eat more, as our hunger is not being satisfied.

We really want to avoid this yo-yoing of blood sugar levels, as not only does it create havoc for our liver and pancreas (diabetes is a disease associated with blood sugar levels), but it massively affects our mood and energy levels.

> "I know that sugar and sweets are not good for me but when I'm at work, the desire to eat them is overwhelming. Last week someone bought a huge packet of 'Percy Pigs' for the team. As they were near my desk, I ended up eating them all and had to rush out and replace them before anyone noticed. While it feels great at the time, I always end up feeling embarrassed and really down afterwards at my greed and inability to stop."
> — Josephine, *Advertising Executive*

It's impossible for us to be effective at work if our blood sugar is careering from high to low.

Low Blood Sugar = Fight or Flight Response

Having low blood sugar is not a fun place to be. As there isn't enough glucose in the blood (which we need to stay alive), our body sees this situation as life-threatening, which it certainly can be, and immediately goes into the flight or fight stress response. Huge amounts of the stress hormones adrenaline are pumped into our blood stream to alert our body that we need to raise our blood sugar immediately to maintain our homeostasis. While we will be unaware of this inner panic, we will experience a range of stress symptoms when we experience low blood sugar levels, that include: anxiety, fatigue, headaches, unable to concentrate, irritability, anger, sweating, and most tellingly, the urge to eat sugary substances immediately.

Essentially experiencing low blood sugar levels is a very powerless place to be: according to one lecture that I attended in Brighton, 80% of criminal activity happens when people have low blood sugar. I'm not saying I am responsible for any local crimes, but I can definitely relate to the lack of restraint when I've got low blood sugar. It doesn't matter if I'm on a health regime or diet; once my blood glucose levels dive then I'm powerless to resist that KitKat Chunky.

The Vending Machine

In my earlier 'less informed' days, one of my work habits was popping down three flights of stairs to the vending machine at around 3pm. Research shows that 11am and 3pm are the times in the day that we are most vulnerable to blood sugar lows. Essentially, for most of us, it's been a few hours since we last ate and is a time when our glucose levels can be waning; while we're not necessarily hungry, we're an easy sell for anything sugary so that we can have a quick pick-me-up. So my afternoon ritual would find me skipping to the huge vending machine to get my KitKat Chunky and packet of Frazzles crisps; it's amazing how soon this changed from being a treat to an everyday necessity. I felt quite hard done by if for any reason I couldn't get this sugary, then salty treat.

While I enjoyed my sugary hit, a few hours later, while driving home I would experience low blood sugar levels again, although I had no idea that this was my physiological state: all I was concerned about was getting another bar of chocolate immediately. Suddenly I would find myself pulling into a local garage in Richmond to gorge on a chocolate bar. This one I wouldn't really even taste, I just needed to eat it quickly. Afterwards, I used to feel quite embarrassed, hiding the sweet wrapper 'evidence' under the car seat and hoping that no one from work saw me guzzling faster than a werewolf on a full moon!

I really believe that if I knew about blood sugar levels then it would have halved my stress levels as rather than thinking I was just greedy with no willpower, I would have realised that something bigger was at play. Having vending machines and access to sugar so readily at work makes restraint harder, especially if your blood sugar levels are yo-yoing. While some of us, are less sensitive to sugar than others and can easily avoid the lure of the chocolate, for some it is much harder. In the book, Prozac Not Potatoes, Dr Kathleen DesMaisons explains that there is a sector of society that is sugar sensitive, meaning that their mood and brain chemistry is much more likely to be adversely affected by sugar.

> "In my sugar eating past, I never understood why I felt so much better after I had candy. I knew it was emotionally comforting, but it didn't make sense that I felt so good after doing something so 'bad'. Sometimes I would binge and start soaring with a sense of possibility about what I could do with my life. I would write plans in my journal, make lists, and feel confident that the world was alright. A few hours later, I would crash and feel like nothing good would ever happen for me, no change would ever come; I would end up a bag lady with nothing to show for my life".
> — Dr Kathleen DesMaisons, Potatoes not Prozac

Alcohol

It's also important to point out that alcohol, as a refined carbohydrate, has a similar affect on our blood sugar levels. While one drink can give us that natural high and the illusion of being able to relax and switch off, the truth is that alcohol actually makes us more stressed-out. The spike in our blood sugar will mean that we'll crave another 'hit', whether that is a drink or sugary food, to maintain the blood sugar high. Also, once we've had a drink, we're more likely to make poor food choices and eat higher amounts of carbohydrates than we would normally.

Symptoms That Your Blood Sugar is Yo-yoing

- See how you answer the following questions:
- Are you rarely wide-awake within twenty minutes of rising?
- Do you need a cup of tea or coffee, a cigarette, or something sweet to get you going in the morning?
- Do you really like sweet foods?
- Do you crave bread, cereal, popcorn or pasta?
- Do you feel you 'need' an alcoholic drink on most days?
- Are you overweight and unable to shift the extra kilos?
- Do you often feel drowsy or sleepy during the day or after meals?
- Do you have mood swings or difficulty concentrating?
- Do you get dizzy or irritable if you go six hours without food?
- Do you find you overreact to stress?
- Do you often get irritable, angry or aggressive unexpectedly?
- Is your energy level now less than it used to be?
- Do you ever lie about how much sweet food you have eaten?
- Do you ever keep a supply of sweet food close at hand?
- Do you get night sweats or frequent headaches?

If you answer yes to eight or more of these questions, then there is a strong possibility that your body is having difficulty keeping your blood sugar level even.

— (Questions from *The 30-Day Fat Burner Diet* by Patrick Holford)

So what to do? Firstly, as always the most important thing is to understand what is going on in your body so that you can then make a decision that is best for you. To lower our stress levels we need to keep our blood sugar levels balanced and we can do this by making some simple food choices. Speaking from my own experience, it's amazing how different you'll feel once your blood sugar is balanced - life really does become different (much better!) without those emotional, powerless highs and lows.

The GI Index

The Glycaemic Index is a good place to start in the blood sugar rebalancing process, as it shows how quickly different foods release sugar into the blood stream: the higher the GI score, the faster the release. It is important to select slow-releasing foods as this will mean that we'll get balanced energy avoiding those emotional highs and lows. The recommendation is that we eat foods with a Glycaemic Index of around 50. Anything with a score of 70 or above should be consumed in moderation or mixed with low GI foods.

So, for example, brown steamed rice has a GI of 50, bulgar wheat has a GI of 48 and oats as a GI of 58. These simple sugars will release slowly into the blood stream. Unsurprisingly, fizzy drinks like Diet Coke or Lucozade have a very high GI as do salty snacks such a pretzels. Much of this is common sense eating where foods that are nearest to their whole, natural state (eg: steamed vegetables and salads) provide the most balanced release of sugar into the blood stream. There is a plethora of information online about how the GI works and how you can create a healthy diet suitable for your own lifestyle.

Bridget's Hunt book *Six Pack Chick* is all about creating a lifestyle that is designed to balance blood sugar levels. It's full of recipes and techniques to keep the blood sugar balanced. She also runs a Facebook community that offers a great support system for anyone who wants to lose weight and have less stress in their lives. An example of what she might eat in one day is listed below.

Breakfast: 2 poached eggs and 2 slices of smoked salmon

Lunch: Big grilled chicken salad with lentils

Dinner: Chilli con carne with steamed broccoli

Snacks: Protein shake at 4pm.

Bridget is a great advocate of eating protein with each meal. Over the years I've really found this useful. The reason why protein is so beneficial is that it slows down digestion as it is broken down in the stomach (unlike carbohydrates which are digested in the small intestine). By combining proteins with carbohydrates we are able to reduce the speed in which glucose enters the blood stream. Good sources of protein include fish, lean meat, eggs, raw nuts, pulses and legumes and seeds.

Breakfast

Having a good protein breakfast is one of the most important things we can do for our blood sugar levels as it really sets up for the day. I know that if I start 'well' with a green juice or avocado on rye bread then I can sail through my day. However if I'm in rush and haven't planned properly I can end up munching through (at least one) bowl of my husband's Crunchy Nut Cornflakes, which are so addictive. For the rest of the day, I'm craving sugary products to replicate that morning high.

"It becomes apparent very quickly that most breakfast cereals are highly-processed carbohydrates. Almost all of these boxed cereals are high glycaemic and have a high glycaemic load – this is not the way you need to start your day. Especially when you consider most people add two pieces of white or wholewheat toast and a glass of orange juice to their breakfast. Kellogg's All-Bran takes the prize when it comes to a highly processed cereal that is both low glycaemic and has a low glycaemic load. If you have ever eaten an All-Bran breakfast you can understand why: it tastes like eating the box. In order for companies to make cereal taste good, they usually need to add a ton of sugar."

— Ray D Strand M.D, Specialist, *Nutritional Medicine*

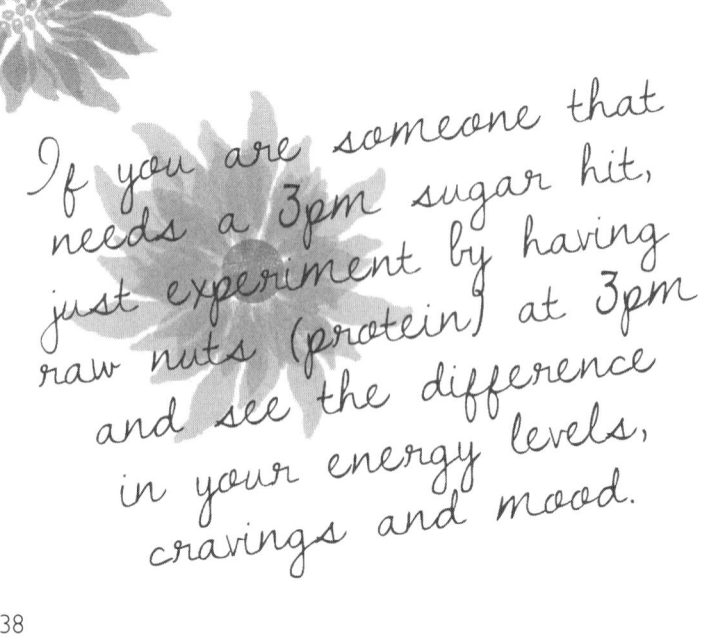

If you are someone that needs a 3pm sugar hit, just experiment by having raw nuts (protein) at 3pm and see the difference in your energy levels, cravings and mood.

Avoid Unnatural Alternatives!

It would be remiss of me to talk about sugar and not mention its clone-like relation - artificial sweeteners. It's really important that we don't replace sugar with sweeteners and we should be very suspicious anytime we see products that claim to be 'sugar free' or have 'no added sugar'. Time and time again I see clients who believe that they are making a healthy choice with a sugar alternative only to cause themselves more problems in the long run. These nasty little manufactured products are often 200 times sweeter than sugar and massively affect our blood sugar levels. They also contain aspartame, which we *really* want to avoid.

The Deal With Aspartame

> "Beyond a shadow of doubt, aspartame triggers brain tumours."
> — The late Dr. M. Adrian Gross, former senior FDA toxicologist

Aspartame is an intense sweetener and is sometimes referred to by its original trade names of Nutrasweet, Equal and Spoonful and it appears on ingredient lists either as 'aspartame' or 'E951'. Aspartame was discovered by accident in 1965 by a chemist from G D Searle Company who was testing an anti-ulcer drug and found it had a very sweet taste. It is made up of 3 chemicals: Aspartic acid, phenylalanine and methanol.

Aspartic acid makes up 40% of aspartame and is an amino acid that has been found to cause serious chronic neurological disorders. Too much aspartic acid in the brain causes cell damage by over-stimulating the cells until they die. Our body's natural defences that eliminate certain toxins like aspartic acid from passing into parts of the brain are not fully developed during childhood, which makes children especially vulnerable to the effects of aspartame. The company who first developed aspartame, the pharmaceutical company, Searle, were warned as far back as 1971 that aspartic acid caused holes in the brains of mice.

Phenylalanine makes up 50% of aspartame. It is an amino acid, like aspartic acid, which transmits impulses in the human brain. Studies have shown that increasing phenylalanine levels in the brain leads to a decreased level of the neurotransmitter serotonin, which can lead to a variety of emotional disorders.

Methanol makes up 10% of aspartame and is a wood alcohol poison. Methanol breaks down into formaldehyde (a known carcinogen), formic acid and diketopiperazine (DKP) which is can contribute to brain tumour development and has also been shown to increase polyps in the uterus and change blood cholesterol levels.

> "I'd been aware of aspartame for some time before I actually started investigating what was in it. I had assumed that as it was included in the food chain that it couldn't be that harmful. I now realise that this type of thinking was completely naive – aspartame is a poison and just shouldn't be included in any ingredients. Personally I think that the diet drinks are the worst, as the caffeine and aspartame combination creates an addictive high. I immediately see the behavioral changes in my children and their friends when they have eaten anything that contains aspartame – they become physically restless, wired, rude to me and aggressive to each other."
> — Claire, *Holistic Practitioner*

You only have to look online to research this topic in more detail – but as many businesses are making a lot of money from aspartame, choose your source of reading material carefully. Whilst I feel strongly that this product should not be part of the food chain, rather than getting ourselves hot under the collar about it, I'd much rather we simply avoid products that contain it.

Embrace Natural Alternatives!

Now we know how unhealthy sugar really is, it is time to embrace the many other products available which are healthy for us and taste SO much better. My all time favourite sweet product of choice is honey. As with any product, we need to be careful where we source it as commercial honey is often treated to make it more liquid which then makes it similar to refined sugar. Ideally we want to go for local, untreated varieties. Much to my husband's delight and often used as an excuse for a visit, our local pub sells honey from neighbouring beekeepers, and it tastes wonderful. While honey does contain more calories than white sugar and still enters our bloodstream quickly, it is also packed full of antioxidants and minerals that in small doses don't upset our blood sugar as much.

Agave syrup is also a good sugar substitute especially in cooking; however – and I can't state this strongly enough – we need to use a natural, organic, unprocessed variety. Sadly there are inferior agave syrups available in the supermarkets that contain fructose which will spike our glucose levels and put us into the fight or flight response. Pure, natural agave has been harvested in Mexico for hundreds of years and made into agave syrup. It has a low GI score and contains fructans that although sounding similar, are very different to fructose. Fructans are 'phytochemicals' with health-giving properties such as being anti-inflammatory and boosting the immune system. Agave syrup has a very sweet taste - a little goes a long way!

Carob is also useful if you want to wean yourself away from chocolate, especially for cooking. This edible bean grows on carob trees from the Mediterranean to the Tropics. While it tastes sweeter than chocolate (reduce the amount required in the recipes) it's has a lower GI score so is good for keeping our stress levels in check.

Don't Beat Yourself Up

My philosophy is to stay as close to nature as possible: natural is always best, and anything highly processed is likely to be less tolerated by the body. I do accept however that this is not always easy to achieve in our fast paced world, and while it definitely helps if I plan my food intake in advance, there are times when I eat sugar and other products that I know aren't always good for me. While in the past I would beat myself up, chastising myself for my lack of willpower – taking away any enjoyment I might have had from the chocolate treat – I now do it differently. If I do eat chocolate, I choose a good quality variety (and enjoy it!) I don't shovel it in quickly, but take time to relish every mouthful.

There have been so many times at work when I've believed, quite wrongly, that something else has caused my stress. While there are some situations that are undoubtedly challenging, they are so much easier to deal with when our blood sugar is balanced and our moods are stable.

Visualisation Exercise

- Close your eyes and take three deep breaths.

- Bring to mind your pancreas - the flat pear shaped organ nestled between the stomach and small intestines on the left side of your body. This organ is responsible for insulin excretion, which controls our blood glucose levels.

- How healthy is your pancreas? What number out of 100, springs into your mind?

- Ask your pancreas what it needs for optimum wellbeing. What is its reply?

Natural Law No. 4

Movement

> *"I have two doctors, my left leg and my right."*
> — G M Trevelyan

This chapter is called 'Move Your Body' rather than 'Exercise' as the latter option in my mind is too closely linked to doing time at a gym. It's so easy for exercise to become yet another thing on the 'To-Do' list, which easily gets forgotten or reprioritised when life gets busy. Over the years I've been a member of lots of different gyms and tried to stay as motivated as possible so that I actually went to them! When I lived in West London, I swapped my membership from my local gym which was a few minutes walk from my house, to the gym that was closer to work. My belief was that I'd get more use from the gym by going before work and during my lunch hour.

Well, I started off fuelled with good intentions, leaving the house at 6am for my pre-work workout. I marvelled at the sun rising and relished having the peaceful commute; I remember thinking "Yes! This is how I want to spend every morning". I even managed to cram in a few lunchtime swimming sessions, sharing the pool with the local OAP swim club who also saw Wednesday at 12.30 as a prime swimming time. All was going well: I definitely felt less stressed, was making better food choices (I even stopped the vending machine run) and I felt more confident at work. This was until a big project was given to me. Suddenly, I was working much longer hours and very quickly didn't have the energy or focus for going to the gym. All my good intentions were quickly forgotten and at a time when moving my body was most needed, it was the first thing that I dropped from my schedule. Steadily my weekdays became more sedentary as I spent the majority of my time sitting at my desk or sitting in my car. I restarted the vending machine visit and ate a lot more sugary products "for energy", and even though I was aware of my rising stress levels, rather than address the issue at that moment, I kept telling myself, as I worked out what I was wasting on my monthly gym membership, that as soon as the project was over, I'd get back into the gym and be 'healthy' once more. I never did.

> "So many people have a misguided mindset that exercise is hard and difficult and then wonder why they are stressed and unfit. We are so lucky that we have such an array of choices open to us. If you like running then run, if you like walking then walk, if you like swimming then swim. It doesn't matter what type of movement you choose to do as long as you enjoy it."
> — Jean-Pierre De Villiers, *The Reshape Coach*.

For many of us, this is so often how exercise at the gym ends up: we start off motivated and then find it hard to sustain in our busy lives. Unless we really enjoy the gym environment or have a firm goal in mind, then all too often it becomes a chore and our initial motivation is lost. So in this chapter we're not talking about going to the gym, we're talking about moving our bodies so that we can have natural wellbeing and less stress in our life. It helps to take a step back and remember why we want to move to our bodies in the first place – if we cast our minds back to Chapter One when we looked at the stress cycle, we saw that it was made up of four parts: the trigger, the hormonal reaction, the physical release and finally rest. While our ancestors engaged with this complete cycle (and were pretty much unaffected by stress), we often get stuck at stage two, having been triggered into fight or flight mode, we're left with the stress hormones, primarily adrenaline, pumping around our blood system. For so many of us at work, once we enter the stress response it can seem like we don't have option for physical release as we're 'trapped' behind our desk, in a meeting room or a traffic jam. So rather than releasing these important stress hormones, we end up suppressing this natural response and with it any uncomfortable emotions; the result being that we're stuck in the stress response for much longer than is necessary. Not good.

"When I'm stressed, I feel like a caged tiger – trapped and angry. It's like there isn't enough space around me and anyone nearby is excruciatingly annoying. Although I stay controlled, I'll shut the desk door really hard or slam the phone down. It doesn't make me feel better though. The only thing that gets rid of this suffocating feeling is going out on my bike. While I may leave the house or office being mad, after a good work out I'll always return much calmer and rational."
— Matthew, *Sales Director*

I'm Pretending To Be Fine

Without movement, feelings and emotions get stuck in our cells, festering away as we stagnate in a murky pool of anxiety.

As we know, when we have adrenaline rushing in our blood stream, our whole mental and physical being is focused on survival, waiting to attack or to be attacked. It's not a comfortable place to be as in many ways we're in lockdown: there is no natural flow or movement, which is vital for homeostatis and wellbeing.

As our body is pumped-up for physical action, blood flow is directed to our muscles, so checking how tight your shoulder and neck muscles are is a good place to start noticing how stressed your body is. As well as the physical tension and pain, we'll also experience this emotionally, as being in fight or flight mode changes us into our 'reptilian shadow' (see Chapter One) as we're operating from the hindbrain, that piece of brain anatomy we share with reptiles that is solely focused on dominance and survival. Through the eyes of our reptilian personality, the world is very different as we're focused on our own survival. We will often disengage from those around us, feeling frustrated and resenting our colleagues. Without movement, these feelings and emotions get stuck in our cells, festering away as we stagnate in a murky pool of anxiety.

Suppress One, Suppress Them All

Movement allows us to let go of suppressed emotions, which is so much better for us than bottling them up. Typically our society puts emotions into 'good' and 'bad' categories - the good ones being happiness, joy, elation (I could go on) and the so-called bad ones which include anger, hatred and frustration. Firstly, we can never suppress just one emotion, so by squashing anger, we also deny ourselves happiness: suppressing one emotion, suppresses them all. And I'd like to add here, there are no bad emotions, they are all part of the same family: we can't experience joy without sadness. It's just repressed emotions that cause us problems as they tend to get bigger the more they are ignored, either leaking out with sharp, barbed comments or exploding in a volcano of anger and resentment when pushed too far.

Adele Theron set up Tantrum Club to specifically create an outlet for suppressed emotions. Her 'Bitch With A Bat' philosophy is gaining huge popularity within the UK as people realise how much better it feels to release stored emotions from the body: www.tantrumclub.com

"I created Tantrum Club so that women can have a place to release all those pent-up emotions. For so long, anger management therapy has focused on talking about our anger rather than expressing it. However, intellectualising our emotions won't release them. Expressing our emotions physically, in a safe space, enables us to get rid of our emotional junk. At Tantrum Club we do that and feel amazing afterwards. By screaming, shouting, ranting, jumping up and down and bashing the living daylights out of sandbags and blocks of ice, we are able to release all of those things that have been waiting to explode out. Tantrum Club and our new fitness programme Tantrum World all seek to express the unexpressed in new and fulfilling ways."
— Adele Theron. Founder, *Tantrum Club and Tantrum World*

Learning From Children

Children are great examples when it comes to releasing stress through moving their bodies. As they live so much more in the moment, they easily glide through the four stages of the stress response and have no problem releasing the stress hormones physically. As children are used to moving around a lot, they don't experience tension and pain like adults do. Typically, children move through the stress cycle (often many times in one day) quite quickly. Once they have expressed their displeasure, they move onto the next emotion without a backward glance, all previous misery forgotten very quickly.

"My brother made me angry when he took the iPad in the middle of my favourite Lego-world game. Mummy told me to go on the trampoline and then I forgot that my brother was naughty."
— Oliver, six-years-old

Unfortunately at work, we can't have a good tantrum even though I believe it would be much healthier for us in the long run if we did! I often think that 'road rage' is an extreme example of people trying to rid themselves of their stress hormones; tension can often build in the body like a pressure cooker until the smallest thing can set it off.

When my husband and I bought the house that we live in now, it needed a lot of work, as the previous owner had not touched it for over twenty years. So for three months, Matt (my husband) and I did a lot of painting and restoring. We spent one long, cold, Saturday wallpaper stripping and painting. I was growing increasingly frustrated that Matt's 'work' kept falling on my head: either paint dripped over me or bits of stripped wall paper was getting stuck in my hair. Rather than dealing with the situation there and then, I suppressed my anger with the belief that I just needed to get the room finished. At 10pm that night, a large chunk of wet, smelly, stripped wallpaper landed in my left eye. Suddenly a day's worth of suppressed emotions unleashed and I erupted. Matt was quite surprised and shocked – he did make the mistake of initially laughing, which didn't help. A torrent of rage emerged from me, completely disproportionate to the situation, and while I dread to think what the neighbours thought, I'm aware that this excessively emotional outburst was really rooted in the fact that I had been rigid the whole day and my repressed stress hormones had been steadily growing.

Letting Go

Rather than become a crazed wild woman, there are many ways that we can release our stress. This does involve movement but is actually much easier and more accessible than you would think. Moving does not mean that you have to do an hour's 'cardio' in the gym – trust me, we can let go much quicker than that, and in a much more fun way.

Immediate Movement Techniques For Work

These are techniques that can be used any time you feel yourself enter the fight or flight response:

Three Deep Breaths

When we're in fight or flight mode, our breath gets very shallow and becomes almost like a pant. By stopping and taking consciously deep breaths, this allows us time to change the internal 'danger' message being sent around our body. Slow breathing calms our central nervous system, taking us out of that state of attack to a calmer, grounded place of reality. It's incredibly simple and effective and can be done anywhere - at your desk, in the car, even during a meeting.

Put both feet on the floor, back straight, close your eyes (if the situation allows) relax and lower your shoulders and inhale inwards through the nose - expanding your stomach - expanding your stomach like a huge balloon. Pause and hold your breath to the count of three and then release slowly, again through the nose. Repeat three times. The longer and slower your in- and out-breaths are, the more effective and stress-releasing this will be.

A variation of this is called 'bee breathing' which was introduced to me by a close friend Danielle Marchant. It's a very simple and a great way to center yourself. Place your thumbs in your ears and your hands facing forward. Your first two fingers then cover your eyes (gently). Take a slow in-breath. On your out-breath you hum. Try at least three rounds of this and notice how you feel afterwards.

The WC – Wall

At work, the WC is an ideal place to release (in every sense of the word!) as it's often the most private space in the building. Depending on how strong the cubicle is, pushing against a wall is a great way to get those hormones out of your body. Stand with your legs equal distance apart and push against the wall really hard. It really helps to vocally express too (although if you're in a shared washroom it may be worth making sure the CEO isn't in the next cubicle). A whispered or even silent "No" under your breath is a great way to express and release those stress hormones. Take a moment to stop, shake your body and repeat twice.

The WC – Shaking

If your local WC is a flimsy set-up and pushing against a wall could have disastrous effects, then shaking your body is just as effective. Shaking is a really old stress techniques and animals from polar bears to rabbits will regularly have a shake to release building tension. It may feel a little weird to start off with but just remember that no one is watching. A good shake-out involves the whole body: start with your hands and feet and build up to the legs, arms and torso. Try not to concentrate when you're shaking – you want to close your eyes, breathe and release all those stress hormones.

Walk Around The Block

When we're in fight or flight mode, sometimes the best thing we can do is remove ourselves from the situation. A change of scene often gives us a change of perspective, so having a quick trot around the block as soon as you enter fight or flight , in my opinion, is worth at least two 'boxercise' classes. The thing to do is go on your own (you don't want anyone to moan to and thus keep you stuck in resentment/anger phase) and walk fast, breathing fresh air in deeply, and actively visualise the stress releasing from your body. You'll naturally start slowing down once you are calmer. Move your shoulders, swings your arms - loosen your body and breathe.

Crying

> "Crying tears is one of the main ways the body can rid itself of toxic hormones which will damage the body if allowed to accumulate"
> — Pip Waller, *Holistic Anatomy*

While it is not encouraged in the workplace, crying is a great way of releasing stress and tension. I studied under Pip Waller, the medical herbalist and shamanic healer for many years and she was a huge advocate of releasing toxicity by having a good weep. She once said that one of the reasons she thought women lived longer than men was because it is more acceptable for women to cry, which ensures that stress hormones are quickly evacuated through body fluids. I know that if I'm upset, having a good cry can make me feel much better. However this can be tricky in the workplace when we're surrounded by other people and more often that not, when we are upset we have to swallow down our tears. If you've had to suppress that lump in your throat then revisiting it, (at a time when you are in the right environment to cry) is hugely beneficial. Watching a film can also help get you back in touch with those repressed feelings. The film Beaches works really well for me: I now only need to hear the intro to 'Wind Beneath My Wings' and I can allow those stress releasing tears to fall.

Laughing

> "I made the joyous discovery that ten minutes of genuine belly laughter had an anesthetic effect and would give me at least two hours of pain-free sleep."
> — Norman Cousins, *Anatomy of Illness*

Laughing is also a wonderful way of releasing stress from the body. When Norman Cousins, an American political journalist was given six months to live, he decided to "die happy" and self-medicated with comedy films and large doses of vitamin C. Rather than die, he fully recovered and attributed a large part of his renewed health to watching Marx Brothers films. Laughing, or as Cousins says "internal jogging" is a great stress release and mood enhancer. United Mind (unitedmind.co.uk) is a company which runs training courses and workshops specifically on laughing. As their statement says: "When you laugh you change. When you change the whole world changes".

Medium-term Movement Techniques

While it may not always be possible to implement these techniques immediately, they don't require any forward thinking so are great when you've had 'one of those days' and want to release any residual stress hormones. These techniques also work better if you state your intention aloud: what you want to release and how you want to feel afterwards.

Vocal Release

We don't often get the chance to really express ourselves and having a good old rant (out of ear-shot of the neighbours) is great for releasing all those negative stuck emotions. I find that the car is a good place as you can really turn up the volume on the radio and go for it. When driving back from work, I used to visualise my 'complex' manager and say everything that I'd been holding in all day. Don't worry if you don't want to form words - noises and groans are just as good. After my release, I felt fantastic afterwards - totally cleansed, having said my piece without any guilt as no one else had been party to my mad rant. Its important that while you go for it, (sometimes this can involve flailing your arms and hands) that you are road safe too. Pulling over to the side of the road can work better in these circumstances.

Punching the Pillow

Start by visualising what you want to release and then start punching a pillow. Having loud music in the background helps. This can tire you out quickly, however persevere so that all those stress hormones have an exit route. Sometimes it can help to have a five-minute break to get your breath back, and then go again. It sounds crazy but it really is an excellent way to release stress!

Vigorous Vacuum Cleaning

I like the vacuum cleaner as it makes a noise and thus covers any ranting and railing that I am making myself. Before you start, visualise the situation and person and state how you wish to feel at the end and then go for it. You may be quite exhausted by the end, but that's no bad thing – and you'll have a cleaner home, which is an additional bonus!

Long-term Movement Techniques

These techniques require a little work before they can be implemented, but can be really useful as part of your regular natural wellbeing maintenance.

Talking

The reason I have included talking in the long-term section is that often when we enter fight or flight mode, an instant response can be to try and release these hormones by having a good moan to the nearest person. This is something that we want to avoid (see Chapter Five) as although it is movement in some form (we are moving our mouths) we're doing it from a stressed state and communicating from our reptilian side, which is never balanced or based in reality.

If we are getting triggered by a recurrent situation, then of course, we do need to address it by talking to the appropriate person, but we should do this *after* we have moved our body. We need to release the stress hormones first by one of the immediate techniques, such as a walk around the block. Once we have less tension and more flexibility we'll be able to express ourselves more clearly, as well as hear what our colleague has to say.

> "I enjoy working with both men and women, however I notice that there are certain traits that women in my team express which, in my opinion, cause them to get stressed. For example, when they are upset with someone, they tell everyone else, getting themselves more worked-up – rather than speaking to the person directly. Talking is so important but it's imperative to learn to talk to the right person."
> — Bradley, *Graphic Designer*

Massage

Massage is fantastic for creating movement especially in areas that are feeling tight and uncomfortable. The reason for this is that massage moves blood (full of oxygen and nutrients) around the body creating flow and balance in areas that can be rigid and stagnant. Having been a massage therapist for many years, I see that there is always a connection between my clients' emotional and physical state. Increasingly massage is becoming popular in the work place as specially designed short sessions can target muscles that become tight from long hours sitting at a desk. I find that office-related tension is mostly found in the shoulders and neck, and if this is not released, then after time it can affect nerve ending in the hands and wrists. If you have a recurring area of pain or tension, there is often a message that your body is trying to reveal. Create some quiet time (the end of a massage is ideal for this) and ask your body what it wants you to know - don't over-think it, trust the first thought that comes into your head.

"There is something magical about massage at work. I often go in for my session feeling 'fine' and it's only afterwards, once the massage is over that I realise my fine was actually pretty tense. During the treatment I notice my mind slowing down too and thoughts and solutions pop into my head effortlessly. If everyone started their day with a massage, there would be no stress."
— Emily, *Personal Assistant*

Walking

In the Morris & Hardman (1997) report 'Walking to Health', the authors state that walking is the nearest activity to perfect exercise. As well as the health benefits, brisk walking is an ideal way to release physical tension. Some people incorporate this into their work day by parking away from the office and walking the last fifteen minutes, or getting off a tube stop earlier. Wear comfortable clothes and shoes and walk with the natural intention that you want to release any stress being held in your body. There are many apps and websites that can show you different walking routes. My favourite sites are walkforlife.info and mapmywalk.com. If you are interested in walking with other people then the website walkingforhealth.org.uk lists where your nearest walking group is located. These regular walks are led by volunteers, who are passionate about walking and getting people outdoors.

Dancing

Dancing is especially good for releasing stress hormones as it involves music, which immediately changes your emotional state. 5 Rhythms dancing, created by Gabriel Roth, uses dance as a form of emotional expression and release. Dancers move through five states - flowing, staccato, chaos, lyrical and stilllness. This sequence is called a 'wave' and lasts an hour. There are no routines and you are encouraged to let your body express whatever it needs to. I found the class incredibly uplifting and once I overcame any self-conscious feelings (closing my eyes helped!) it was one of the most stress-releasing experiences of my life. The Mental Health

Organisation did a research project on this type of dance and found it to be a particularly effective form of stress management. For more information or to find out where your local class is, look at gabrielroth.com

> "Dancing matters because it's soul food. We hunger for ecstasy, for that quiet disappearing act when whoever we think we are turns into all that we can be. It doesn't matter if you dance in the subway, in the backseat of a car, on a rooftop, in a grocery line, in a room by yourself, or in a room of spinning bodies. What matters is that we keep moving and spurring each other on into the depths of our creativity and originality, to be imaginative and a little bit wicked".
> — Gabriel Roth, *blog*

Yoga

There are many different types of yoga from the slower *hatha* to the more demanding *ashtanga*. Yoga is so flexible now that you can do it in a way that suits you: from finding a local class to buying a DVD or even looking on YouTube for a post-work yoga routine. Many companies see the benefits that yoga can offer to their employees and run classes during lunch hours or after work. Doing exercise at work is great way to recharge during the working day and having it at your workplace means that you are more likely to attend regularly. Even if your company doesn't currently offer yoga classes, it's always worth speaking to your HR department to see if you can organise a weekly class. All that is required is a large meeting room and a yoga teacher. The British Wheel of Yoga (www.bwy.org.uk) has a list of yoga teachers in your area.

While there are many different choices for movement, the most important thing is that you choose some form of movement that works for you. Unless it's enjoyable then it won't be sustainable and as soon as you get busy at work then it will be first thing that gets dropped. Often the times when our bodies most need movement is when we least feel like doing anything. However busy we are, we can all find twenty minutes a day to move. Yes, it can take discipline but remember that when it comes to exercise, 'little and often' makes a HUGE difference to our stress levels and our natural wellbeing.

Our bodies were not designed to sit all day, they were made to move, so opt for the more active path when you can: walk up those escalators, choose the stairs rather than the lift or just get active in front of the TV. Your body and health will thank you for it.

Visualisation Exercise

- Close your eyes and take three deep breaths:

- Imagine a cluster of stress hormones in your body – they can appear anyway you choose.

- Ask these cells what form of physical exercise they want to take in order to leave your body.

- What type of exercise do they choose?

- Take your time to imagine them enjoying their exit route whether they are running, swimming or even cycling out of your body.

Natural Law No. 5

Tolerance

> "No man is an island, entire of itself."
> — John Donne

The relationships we have at work can so often have the biggest impact on our stress levels. For the majority of us, we spend more time with our colleagues than anyone else. Report after report states that positive relationships with our co-workers will keep us in a job for longer and produce better results, while bad office dynamics will make us stressed-out, unhappy and depressed. And in my experience this is true. When I have worked in companies where there is good team rapport, work feels less like work: I looked forward to going in each morning and as my confidence was higher I achieved more positive outcomes. However when I've worked in places when there is not a good team atmosphere, then very quickly Sunday night can often be the worst time of the week as the thought of going in the next day can be sickening. This is definitely not the ideal foundation for natural wellbeing.

> "The fashion industry is renowned for its 'divas' however I had never realised the impact that one person could have on me. After a successful career as a buyer for over ten years I was really happy with how my career was progressing. However, when a new Director was brought in from a rival firm, everything changed. She had a reputation for being a nightmare and made the character that Meryl Streep played in 'The Devil Wears Prada' look like a mouse. Everything changed: she micro-managed, undermined my confidence and made negative comments about my own personal

style. She constantly changed decisions and made sure she took credit for my work. After six months of being miserable and upset, I handed in my notice."
— Chrissy, *Fashion Buyer*

Life is just too short to feel miserable at work. While some people can be blissfully unaware and unaffected by other people's mood and behaviour, for many of us, how our colleagues and managers act all too often impacts our working and home life. Cultivating good relationships with our colleagues makes a huge difference as it can help reduce our stress levels and create natural wellbeing, especially for women. John Gray the author of *Men Are From Mars, Women Are From Venus* says that when under stress, men typically tend to retreat and cut off from those around them, however when women are stressed, they often need to talk about problems to help alleviate the stress.

In her book *The Tending Instinct*, Shelley E Taylor, a psychology professor at the University of California states that while men and women both undergo the same physical experiences of stress, men predominately exhibit the fight (aggression) and flight (social withdrawal/isolation) response, while women often followed a 'tend and befriend' model to deal with high levels of stress. Her research highlights how important social interaction and support is for many people, especially women. Research undertaken by the *Gallop Business Journal* also reveals that employees who have best friends at work identify significantly higher levels of healthy stress management. Regardless of gender, I believe that we all benefit form having someone to talk to in the workplace.

However, it's important to be discerning with your choice of confidant. While we all have different boundaries with those around us, some of us are happy to create work friendships that go outside of the office while others prefer to keep a separation between work and home. It's important to remember that whatever the office culture, the usual social norms don't apply with work colleagues purely because in many ways we're in an unnatural environment. As our moral compasses are all set differently, expecting people to behave in a certain way (especially at work) is a fast track to disappointment.

I used to have one manager that I found very tricky to work for purely because I used to take his behaviour personally. One moment he would be in an upbeat, jovial mood, sharing confidences with me, and just as quickly his mood would darken and all communication would be cold as he distanced himself from me, and the team. I found that *I* changed according to his mood swings: when he was upbeat so was I; when he was distant and cold, so was I. Not only was my emotional mirroring tiring but I let my enjoyment of my job be dependent on whether he was in a good mood.

To harvest good office vibes, there are three useful guidelines to follow:

The Three Golden Rules for Good Working Relationships

Golden Rule No. 1: Be discerning

Take your time regarding who you choose to have in your inner circle. It doesn't necessarily have to be the person that you sit next to or work with. As Jon Rohn, the self-made millionaire states, "We are the average of the five people that we spend the most time with," so think carefully about the qualities that you want to portray and look at who emulates them in your office. Just because you sit next to someone, it doesn't mean that you have to spend all your time with them. Suzanne Hazelton in her book *Great Days At Work* talks about making a bid when you wish to initiate friendship within the workplace. "In the world of relationships, nothing happens until someone makes a bid... equally important in the bidding process is the response we get to our bids. If the other party does not respond by paying attention to our bid in a positive way, the game stops, like a ball that dies when a tennis serve is not returned. Unlike the tennis serve, the goal of the bid is not to defeat the opponent but to encourage a volley." (Ulrich and Ulrich, 2010)

Golden Rule No. 2:
Don't moan/bitch/put-down about another colleague

However exasperating, difficult or downright rude a colleague may be - NEVER moan about them to someone you work with. Although it can create an initial bonding, building a relationship based on alienating another is not a good foundation for good communication in the workplace. While it can be tempting it is just not worth it in the long run – you never know who is listening or if and when your comments will be repeated.

At a company where I worked, one of my colleagues overheard two people that she worked closely with talking about her in the adjoining meeting room. While not all of it was negative, she was so upset to be dissected in this way that the team dynamic was never quite the same afterwards.

If you are surrounded by difficult colleagues, take (silent) comfort in the knowledge that other people will no doubt feel exactly the same way. Implement some of the 'Move Your Body' techniques in Chapter Four to naturally release any of those negative feeling associated with these people. Vigorous vacuuming or punching the pillow when you get home can be particularly effective in these circumstances.

Golden Rule No. 3:
Confront the issue

The intensity of the office environment can mean that people behave in ways that do not always show their best side. Deadlines, difficult clients or problems at home impact us all differently, so it's important not to take it personally. If someone has noticeably changed in their attitude towards you or behaves rudely or aggressively, it's crucial to deal with the issue rather than ignore what's going on. This may be harder for some of us – it just depends on how comfortable you are with confrontation. While there are times when I have dreaded bringing up an issue, I find the more I practice confronting difficult situations, the easier it gets. Try to remember that, for some reason the person in question is operating from their reptilian mindset. Find specific examples and then say how it made you feel.

> "Statements of opinion are always more constructive in the first person 'I' form. Compare these two statements: 'You never take my suggestions seriously' and 'I feel frustrated that you have not responded to my last four e-mails, which leads me to believe that my suggestions are not that important to you. Is that so?' The former can elicit a quick and defensive 'That's not true!' The latter is much harder to deny. One triggers a disagreement; the other sparks a discussion."
> — Sheryl Sandberg, *Lean In*

Clearing up misunderstandings is crucial if we wish to stay balanced in the workplace and while it can be easier to hide behind an email, effectively building relationships when an issue arises can only be resolved through face-to-face communication.

Email Etiquette

While email is great for specific work-related actions, it falls short when dealing with personal issues or difficult subjects, and so often an innocent email can cause unintentional hurt especially if it is written in a hurry. *Never send an email in a hurry or when you're angry.* Always re-read your email critically and if forwarding an email, check that there is nothing offensive included. I once had a manager who forwarded an email that at the bottom had included a comment to his friend that myself and another co-worker were "playing up and needing whipping into shape". Speaking from experience, I'd say that these scenarios should be avoided if you want to get the best from your team!

Never send an email when you're angry!

Staying Balanced

Staying balanced around others is not always easy, especially if you work with someone that is particularly negative. In working teams, we can often come across someone that could be described as a bad apple or an energy drain – that one person who negatively impacts and 'brings down' the rest of the team. I went to a talk once and the speaker described it slightly more graphically as a "turd in the swimming pool!" He asked a packed auditorium who would jump into a swimming pool if there was a turd in it. Interestingly about eight people put their hands up. However the majority of us wouldn't as the turd had contaminated the whole pool.

Often the apples, drains or turds (whichever description you prefer) aren't aware of their contaminating affect. As we can't choose who we sit near or work with, it can be tricky if you're next to a bad apple as they like to draw people in to agree with their opinions and judgments. The rule of not taking them personally is essential here and in some cases may mean that we have to create boundaries as well as change our mindset around a particular person.

Creating Boundaries

Creating boundaries means different things to different people. Although it can sound physical, it's not about creating physical (or even emotional) constraints, but essentially it's about maintaining your identity and staying true to yourself. In many situations I find this relatively easy, but when I'm tired or around strong, forceful people then my boundaries can become much weaker and before I know it I've said yes to something or agreed with an opinion that isn't true for me. While I would no doubt choose to avoid being around challenging people in my ideal world, life doesn't always allow us this luxury and having learnt the hard way, it's actually good for us to practice having good strong boundaries. The most important thing is to be clear and detached. Have a few stock phrases at hand that can be helpful in establishing your boundaries, such as "I appreciate how you might feel about that," or "That's interesting, but I had a different experience to that".

I very much like the work of William Bloom and his attitude towards creating and maintaining personal boundaries. In his book *Psychic Protection* he talks about creating a protective bubble or egg around yourself – this is probably one of the most well-known forms of boundary setting and one that I use regularly if I'm aware that my boundaries need boosting.

Bubbles Of Protection - a short meditation

- Get comfortable and relaxed

- Earth yourself and guide your breath into a comfortable and relaxed rhythm

- Imagine and sense that you are surrounded by a transparent protective bubble or egg, which protects you from negative vibrations

- Spend a while sensing this bubble all around you: over your head; under your feet; completely protecting your back; completely surrounding you.

- Sense that your own vibrations can exit through the membranes of the bubble.

- Sense that the bubble does not prevent good energies from coming in.

- Be very relaxed and comfortable in it.
    — (*Taken from Psychic Protection* by William Bloom).

This is just a guide: some people prefer to work with colours or symbols when it comes to maintaining boundaries – use your imagination and experiment; go with whatever works best for you.

"I've always been sensitive to other people's moods so each morning, before I walk into the office, I mentally step into my bubble of light. It sounds really odd saying it out loud but I've been doing it for years. Being in my safety bubble means that it doesn't matter who I am around and how stressed out they are, I won't soak up their energy. When the atmosphere at work is particularly manic, I find myself mentally scanning my bubble to check there aren't any holes!"
— Emily-Jane, *Travel Advisor*

Another tried and tested technique that I use a lot is shifting my mindset. It's so easy to judge someone when they act in a way that we wouldn't, so as soon as I find myself thinking "I would NEVER do that" – it's time to shift my mindset.

Changing Your Mindset

Jack Canfield, author of *Chicken Soup For The Soul* illustrates this really well when he talks about being on a train early one Sunday morning. While sitting on the train reading his book and enjoying the peace, a man with five children got on. Immediately the whole peaceful atmosphere changed as the children were loud, shouting and running across the other seats. Throughout the time, the father just sat there and said nothing. Jack Canfield, annoyed at the interrupted peace, started to judge the father and after ten minutes of inward seething he mentioned the noise and 'wild' behaviour. The father looked up and replied quietly by saying that he was sorry, but they had just left the hospital where his wife, the children's mother, had died.

As soon as Jack knew the man's story, all the judgment that had been building up, fell away. Instead he felt huge amounts of compassion and wanted to help this man that only a few minutes ago he was feeling angry towards. Remembering this can really help when dealing with our colleagues. We never know what is going on for them and while their outward behaviour may be challenging, we don't know their story or what other factors are going on in their life that is causing them to behave in this way.

> "I've always enjoyed the friendships that I make at work and at my last company, our department used to work really well together. However there was one colleague who was cold and distant. She never asked anyone how they were and only made tea and coffee for herself. However on an 'away day' she shared that she had a disabled son. Suddenly my whole attitude changed towards her and rather than feeling vague annoyance I felt huge compassion. Once I knew this, I always went out of my way to make her life easier."
> — Adrienne, *Legal Secretary*

This point brings me to the third section of the chapter on 'Not Taking It Personally'. We are all so different and when we're stressed and in the hindbrain, reptilian mindset, we take on characteristics that are hard for others to understand. I often see five different types of 'animal behaviour' that colleagues can use as a 'default' when stressed. As well as noticing this in ourselves, it can really help to see which 'animal' our colleagues revert to as another tool for not taking it personally. While people may change their animal type, we will often find at work that there is one dominant type that certain colleagues will revert to if triggered into the stress response.

The Roaring Lion

The roaring lion is the easiest response to spot as it is the most vocal of all the animal behaviour. The voices of these 'types' naturally tend to be loud and it is hard to miss it when a lion gets angry or upset. These types are naturally positive and have high self-esteem, so any affront to their ego whether it be a direct insult or an encounter with rudeness (these types hate bad manners) can be a stress trigger in the lion's world. As the lion is symbolic of the sun, these types feel the heat and tend to perspire more than any of the other types.

If You Are A Roaring Lion
If you find yourself triggered then the best tactic is to close your mouth and head to a mirror – take some time to connect with yourself in the mirror, breathing deeply and reminding yourself of all your natural qualities and abilities.

If Your Colleague Is A Roaring Lion
Let them roar and give them ample time to get it off their chest. Once they have expressed their annoyance it will often pass very quickly. Don't interrupt them or play devil's advocate. Acknowledge the good qualities that you see in them and appreciate their 'roaring' qualities are a stress outlet for them.

The Lonely Mole

The lonely mole types tend to disappear into a dark hole when they are stressed and distance themselves from others. There is an overriding sense they want to be alone to sort out the issue and anyone trying to talk to them is seen as an additional unwanted annoyance. Lonely moles don't see that when they come up from the dark hole, the situation is never has overwhelming as they feared, and that by sharing or delegating the problem could have been resolved effortlessly.

If You Are A Lonely Mole
If you notice yourself sliding into a tunnel to be alone, remind yourself that this is not the best strategy to solve the issue at hand. Take three deep breaths and repeat the affirmation "I am open to accepting and receiving support".

If Your Colleague Is A Lonely Mole
Rather than try to talk to them, lonely moles will respond much better if you do something for them such as get them a glass of water. Ideally getting these types outside into the fresh air and sunlight will work wonders, as the sunlight reminds these moles that they don't have to retreat into their holes alone to get the job done.

The Scared Deer

The scared deer type can be recognised by a panic-stricken 'eyes caught in the headlights' expression; they are often pale in appearance and breathe very shallowly. This overall sense of being paralysed is due to feeling overwhelmed and overburdened, and not being sure where to start as it all seems 'too much'. This panicked state can often be triggered by the person being given an additional task – it just overwhelms them. Although scared deer are very capable, they are often perfectionists and fearful of making mistakes which can mean that their work takes longer to complete. Scared deer feel the cold more than other types as the body can enter a state of shock.

If You Are A Scared Deer
Firstly try to start breathing deeply – this increases the blood flow to your brain and allows the panicky, rigid feeling to dissipate. Affirmation: "I am doing the best I can, and that is fine".

If Your Colleague Is A Scared Deer
Scared deer respond very well to support and often a positive comment can work wonders. Sitting down with a scared deer to plan their day can help unlock the paralysis and help them see their workload is manageable.

The Drowning Duck

In many ways the drowning duck is the hardest type to spot as on the surface, everything looks fine: the drowning duck gives the impression that everything is in control and on target. These types are often seen as pillars of strength and can take on caring roles, but it is when too much has been taken on that the duck types feel pulled down. A duck in drowning mode can be detected though body language. Clues to notice are lack of eye contact, lack of humour and this normal upbeat duck becoming quiet and more serious.

If You Are A Drowning Duck
Stop and ask for help. Sharing problems is not a sign of weakness and unless you prioritise your own needs first, you will be unlikely to support any others. Affirmation: "Asking for and receiving help is a sign of strength".

If Your Colleague Is A Drowning Duck
As drowning ducks can be scared to vocalise any weaknesses, it is important that any communication does not imply that they cannot cope. Asking them what support they need can work well.

The Mute Mouse

The mute mouse is the type that finds any form of confrontation very difficult. Although not necessarily quiet in life, being in a situation where they have to stand-up for themselves or speak about something that is upsetting them is very challenging for this type. Rather than deal with the problem directly their downfall is that they talk to everyone else (often at length) about the person or issue rather than confronting the person involved. Often mute mice can have sore throats or notice that when they are feeling under the weather, their glands become swollen.

If You Are A Mute Mouse
Remember that dealing with the issue directly will be much more beneficial than any avoidance tactics. Visualise yourself having the conversation in advance, starting the conversation with "When you did xxx, I felt xxx". By practicing in advance, it will enable any emotional charge to be released and is less likely to include repressed emotions.

If Your Colleague Is A Mute Mouse
Do not fight their battles. Encourage them to stand up for themselves and deal with the person in hand. While being supportive, do not sympathise, as sympathy is not a long-term strategy to effectively address the issues mute mice experience.

In general, if you are having issues with a colleague, don't think that you have to sort it out immediately. Responding from a stressed, attacking state or from our default animal stereotype can make situations worse. As mentioned earlier, one of the best things that we can do is communicate, but to ensure that we are coming from a calm and open space we need to prepare ourselves:

The Invisible Conversation

This technique is effective when you have stored anger towards a particular colleague. Find a quiet, private place to do this exercise and after settling yourself, imagine the person in front of you. Take some time to really bring them into focus and without censoring yourself, tell them exactly what you think of them. Let it all out and use as many expletives as necessary. The important part is to release all the tension from your body. Once you have expressed fully, tell them how you want to move forward in this working relationship. (Keep breathing!) Visualise a new scenario between you both.

This technique also works effectively as a letter. Find a quiet, private place to write down all the resentment and upset that you have been feeling. Once you have emptied yourself emotionally, it is important to dispose of the letter afterwards either by burning it, shredding it or even tearing it up and flushing it down the toilet.

Three Positive Traits

Another tactic that I find useful when preparing for 'colleague communication' is to think about three positive traits that they have. Initially it's easy to think that they don't have any, but this is never the case – everything is a balance and by acknowledging three positive traits in them, it helps to loosen the rigid mindset that we can get into. It also helps to look at their behaviour and ask ourselves if we have done a similar thing, or behaved in the same way? This develops empathy and a deeper awareness that our colleagues may be in the stress response themselves.

Visulisation Exercise

- Close your eyes and take three deep breaths:

- Imagine that you are looking down at your body from the outside.

- Notice if there are any attachment cords connecting you to anyone or attached to you from someone else. These cords are depleting your energy so take your time to scan your body and see where they are placed.

- Trust your intuition.

- When you see any cords, what type of material they are made up of?

- Take a cutting instrument of your choice and cleanly cut through any cords which are binding you to another person.

- Release the attachment and mentally close any holes that these cords may have left.

Natural Law No. 6

Beginning

> "A journey of 1,000 miles begins with a single step."
> — Lao-tzu

One of the biggest causes of stress at work is procrastination: putting-off those tasks that seem difficult or overwhelming. It doesn't seem to matter if it's a huge project, a small task or a phone call – when we try and avoid anything, rather than it going away, the pressure only builds and the issue gets bigger and more insurmountable in our minds. Consciously ignored issues seem to create a life of their own, stalking us throughout the day as they hover in the back of our minds, reminding us of their existence especially when we're trying to switch off from work.

There was one particular project that really stands out for me, when I displayed all the typical procrastination signs. At the time, I was working for a multi-national company and there were three operating companies in the UK. One of the operating companies decided to create a project aimed at independent retailers and while this was not my area of expertise at all, I had been chosen as the lead from my particular business. Part of this project was a press week that I was given sole responsibility for and with an already busy workload and a lack of direction and understanding of where to start, I became increasingly overwhelmed and resentful of the project. Procrastination set in.

Every time an email (and believe me there were lots) flew into my inbox, I felt a surge of anger and quickly hid the offending item in a sub-folder. I jumped upon any reason not to start and I became really 'busy' focusing on other, less important jobs, following up on unimportant enquiries, and my desk had never been so tidy! Even though I was looking super-busy to the outside world, the more I ignored this project, the more heavily it played on my mind both inside and outside of work. Once, I woke up in the middle of the night, thinking about the looming press week having just dreamt that all my teeth were crumbling. It was not good. Each day 'Sort Out Press Week' would be at the top of my 'To-Do' list and yet I'd leave work with this task not even started and as a result, feel stressed and cross.

The interesting thing was that as soon as I took the first step (opening the emails) and broke down the task into small chunks, identifying the people I needed to speak to and working out a time line; it was actually quite simple. My mood massively changed and my stress levels reduced purely because I had come out of a stagnant procrastination state and just started! By finally, pro-actively working on the project, it actually turned out to be (dare I say it), enjoyable.

There are many different reasons why we procrastinate: often it's because the task seems too big, or involves something new and therefore judged by our brain to be 'difficult'. For me it was because the project seemed overwhelming, each email snowballed my feeling of being out of control and incompetent. However rather than admit to any of this, I relied upon my tried and tested procrastination get out clause of 'being too busy'.

In the modern workplace, there is no denying that for most of us there is a lot to do and not enough time to do it. We could be at work 24/7 and still not feel on top of our workload. Unfortunately this is the reality of modern working life. Now, the blessing and curse of having a long, extended 'To-Do' list, is that its very easy to pick and choose what we do first and it's all too easy to go for the easiest option, rather than diving headlong into the hardest tasks first. While this may not look like procrastination – it's not as if we're chewing on our pens, staring out of the window – it definitely is procrastination as in effect, we are putting off anything that we don't want to do, and that ultimately creates stress in our life.

> *There is nothing as difficult or as uncomfortable as procrastination!*

So whether we're aware of it or not, there are some subtle signs that can help us identify if we're procrastinating. Of course, we'll all have different tactics depending on where we work, but on the whole look out for the following activities:

Signs that we're avoiding something

- Taking snack breaks (a lot)
- Taking tea/coffee breaks (a lot)
- Checking emails (a lot)
- Going to the bathroom (a lot)
- Looking at Facebook (a lot)
- Talking (a lot)
- Thinking "I'll do this first, then I'll do ..." (a lot!)

While these activities are innocent enough, when we start doing *a lot* of anything it's often because we are trying to fill our time, avoiding something. I really believe that there is nothing as difficult or as uncomfortable as procrastination. Brian Tracy in his book *Eat That Frog* quotes from Mark Twain who says that if we start our day eating a live frog then nothing worse can happen! Tracy states that we need to start our day by 'eating the frog,' which for us means tackling that hardest, most important task first. Anything else is pure and simple avoidance. Having followed this advice for a number of years now, I know it makes such a difference, not just in the success of my business but the enjoyment of my day-to-day life. Rarely is anything as difficult or unpleasant as I imagine it to be and there is a natural high that comes once I have eaten my frog first thing.

As well as advising us to eat frogs, Brian Tracy states that the key to success (the opposite of procrastination) is to concentrate single-mindedly on the most important task, to do it well and finish it completely. Now, this can be quite tricky at work when there are interruptions and differing demands on our time, but nothing feels better than successfully completing a challenging task.

However, with so many different tasks to do, it can be hard to know which frog needs to be eaten first! To keep our stress levels down and create natural wellbeing one of the first things we need to do is be clear with what we should be focusing our time on. To know this, we need to be adept at prioritising our workload.

The key to success is to concentrate single-mindedly on the most important task.

Prioritising

Being able prioritise is a very important and necessary skill in today's business world. As already mentioned, our work reality is that we'll never get to the bottom of our 'To-Do' list. There will always be something outstanding; something that requires our attention and we need to know how to work out quickly what is important and what isn't. When we don't prioritise our work, we can end up spending our precious time doing low-value tasks which have little long term consequence. Just because something is time consuming, that doesn't mean that it's important or even necessary.

When I first started working in public relations, I was given lots of time-consuming jobs – random things that popped into my manager's head. As I never knew (or asked) how important or time critical the job was, I assumed, in my 'newbie', keenness that everything was important and needed to done immediately. I once stayed until midnight (did I mention that I was keen?) stuffing press releases into envelopes only to find in the morning that the release date had already been delayed for a month.

Now, while I felt important and useful to be seen being busy, rushing round the office at 100mph and having smoke billowing off my keyboard, unless I was dealing with the most important jobs first then this 'small stuff' was mostly meaningless. I started work at the same time as another graduate and she had a very different strategy: whereas I was working long hours and constantly rushing, she was much calmer, and focused most of her time on building press relations which, as we were working in public relations really was most important. It was a great, early lesson to learn as when it came to our six monthly review meeting (which strangely they did together), she could show exactly what benefit she was adding to the business with her contacts and press relationships whereas I, who had put many more hours in, had very limited long term 'worthy' activities to report.

So to ensure that we're eating the correct frog, we need to always be clear about what is expected of us and what specific results we are being judged upon. While many companies factor in six-monthly or yearly reviews, don't be afraid to book more regular sessions with your manager, especially if you have the type of job that means that different people make demands on your time. Ask your manager for help prioritising your tasks (remember, asking for help is NOT a sign of weakness) and get feedback from them regularly to ensure you are correctly focused.

Saying No

Part of priortising can involve saying "No" if you are asked to work on something that is going to be time consuming and takes you away from your normal day to day work role. Saying no can feel uncomfortable but it's no use agreeing to work if you can't fulfill it or it's going to take you away from critical business tasks. Obviously if it's your boss making this request then this doesn't necessarily apply although it would be advisable to talk to them about your workload and ask for some advice in prioritising if you are expected to take on this extra role; also, if the extra work will give you valuable experience and you are happy and able to put in the required additional time, then again you may decide not to say no.

Saying no does not need to be difficult: it's not being rude, especially it you say why honestly and openly (rather than going through a long list of excuses). You can always advise and support teams and projects without taking on specific time-consuming actions.

Plan Your Day

Planning your day is critical when you want to make the most of your work time and avoid procrastination. While there are always things that may happen during the day to change it, by starting each day with a clear plan it's so much easier to achieve your desired results. Research says that if we spend just ten minutes planning our day then we are likely to save ourselves a good two hours – a great time investment! I always think that planning is most effective if we do it the day before so that our subconscious mind can then get working on finding solutions and making our tasks as seamless as possible. Spending time at the end of your working day is ideal as you can set everything up ready for morning action. Coming into the office to a tidy desk and a clear outline is very productive.

Research says that if we spend just ten minutes planning our day then we are likely to save ourselves two hours.

Planning ahead gives us two advantages: firstly, you can tailor your workload to how *you* work best. Most of us are more productive in the morning and are thus primed and ready for our frog. Afternoons, when our energy can naturally wane, are ideal for activities such as research, planning, and telephone calls. While we can't necessarily choose when we have work meetings, they are much better to be planned in the afternoon rather than occupying prime frog-eating time.

The second advantage planning gives us is that we can break down our tasks into manageable and realistic activities. As I know only too well, getting started can be held up when we're not sure where to start. I find the saying, 'How do you eat an elephant? One bite at a time!' really useful when I find that I'm stuck in overwhelm. As soon as I changed 'Sort Out Press Week' on my To Do list into smaller bite size pieces then suddenly this daunting proposition seemed very possible. Mark Twain says it so much more eloquently than me: "The secret of getting ahead is getting started. The secret of getting started is breaking your complex overwhelming tasks into small manageable tasks and then starting on the first one."

Stay Focused!

There are many distractions in the office – so much so that it's very easy to get pulled off track by emails, phone calls or people just wanting to ask us questions (or gossip!). When we're eating our frog or focusing on any task, we enter a deep level of concentration that allows us to focus all our creativity and brain cells on that specific task at hand. Every time we get interrupted from that deep concentration zone, it will take us at least seven minutes to get back there. This can really add up and makes finishing tasks much longer and more drawn out than they should to be.

There seems to be an unwritten rule many of us follow, that we need to respond to emails or calls or texts immediately. This just isn't the case – there is rarely anything so important that it can't wait at least an hour. It's practically impossible to get jobs finished quickly and well when we regularly get distracted by emails and start multi-tasking, doing all sorts of things at the same time. Contrary to popular belief, multi-tasking is not an effective way of working, as to do any job well, we need to focus solely on it and either complete all of it or part of it before we move onto the next activity.

So, putting the phone onto voicemail and logging-out of your email account for short amounts of time really allows us to really concentrate. Allocating parts of our day to emails and calls works so much better as we can group all communication together. Do not succumb to the lure of email!

There seems to be an unwritten rule that we need to respond to emails or texts immediately – but we should not!

Don't Waste Time! – or, avoid digital distraction

'Don't waste time!' is the best friend of 'Stay focused!' as they are both closely linked. I always find it interesting how different time can sometimes feel in one single day. Although there are always the same number of hours in the day and the same number of minutes in an hour, when I'm in action mode, time flies and before I know it, hours have passed. However when I'm in procrastination mode, it can seem the opposite as the hands of the clock look static and it can feel like I have too much time on my hands. To move time forward I can end up embracing idle conversations with colleagues, checking my emails every few minutes and entering the ultimate in time-wasting activities, looking at Facebook.

Facebook deserves special mention of it's own as of all the social media platforms, this is without doubt the most time wasting one of them all and should be limited to no more than once a day. The Internet can be an incredible time drain if we allow it to be. While it offers a great wealth of information, unless we are clear as to the information we require, we can end up wasting many hours in cyberspace with little to show for it. 'Freedom' is a great app used by the likes of Nick Hornby, Seth Godin and Naomi Klein which allows you to log off from the internet for specific amounts of time which you decide upon. www.macfreedom.com/

Stop Being A Perfectionist

Another reason that procrastination happens and things take longer than they should is that we're in perfectionist mode. While being a perfectionist has some advantages, on the whole it can be a real hindrance as it massively slows down results and holds us back from completing a task. Getting things done well and quickly is much, much better than getting things done perfectly.

> "One of my favourite posters at Facebook declares in big red letters, 'Done is better than perfect'. I have tried to embrace this motto and let go of unattainable standards. Aiming for perfection causes frustration at best and paralysis at worst."
> — Sheryl Sandberg, *Lean In*

I used to sit next to someone who was fantastic at just getting things done. She had her 'To-Do' list for the day planned out and she steadily worked her way through it, ticking off each action as she went. I never saw her get sidetracked or stressed for that matter; she just started whatever was on the top of her list and worked down, doing everything to the best of her ability. There was one time she was writing a press release and once she had drafted it, she sent it over to me to read and give her feedback. I remember reading it and thinking how it still needed quite a lot of work. However I had completely missed the point: while I was huffing and puffing over my release which, due to my perfectionism was taking all afternoon, she had compiled hers, never expecting the first draft to be perfect. Then, based on my feedback she made improvements and finalised it. The whole turnaround was so much quicker than the complicated task I was making a mess of. While it is important to set the bar high, getting things completed 'well and quickly' is much more useful than 'slow and perfect'.

> "My mum has always been amazingly organised — no matter how busy she was, she always used to say that 'there was time for everything' and I've found that I've followed in her footsteps. While I see some colleagues struggle with managing their workloads, I've always found it quite easy just to get on with it. While my 'To-Do' list is flexible, having it as a day-to-day structure means that my important tasks are always prioritised."
> — Justine, *Events Manager*

The simple truth is that avoidance leads to stress. We simply can't have natural well being in the workplace if we're procrastinating over something. The simple step of just starting shifts us from this place of stagnation into a place of action. It's very easy to have excuses and reasons as to why things haven't been done and in some cases we may even believe them ourselves. However regardless who buys into our plethora of reasons and excuses, we always know deep down when we've been procrastinating and have left things to the last minute. While there is nothing like an impending deadline to get us going, starting earlier and planning to finish well in time will keep us much more balanced in the office.

The simple truth is that avoidance leads to stress.

Leaving tasks to the last minute creates a rollercoaster of stress (which is so often accompanied by other stress-inducing habits such as forgetting to drink water, eating sugary snacks and not moving our bodies). Like all habits, avoidance and procrastination can be reversed; research has proved that people's best work is not done at the eleventh hour, moments before the deadlines expire – our best work is done when we've planned for it and set time aside to just get started.

Visualisation Exercise

- Close your eyes and take three deep breaths:

- Bring to mind someone who you admire for being successful and getting things done. They can be alive or dead and you do not have to have known them personally. Have a clear picture of your chosen guide.

- See yourself at work when you're procrastinating. Imagine the person sitting next to you at your desk. What advice do they have for you? How can you do things differently?

- Use this exercise anytime you feel stuck or overwhelmed at work – ask your guide for help and see what suggestions they offer.

Natural Law No. 7

Pause

> "Sit quietly for now and cease your relentless participations. Watch what happens. The birds do not crash out of the sky in mid-flight after all. The trees do not wither and die; the rivers do not run red with blood. Life continues to go on."
> — Elizabeth Gilbert, *Eat Pray Love*

It may seem strange that we jump from the last chapter that is all about getting started, to this chapter that is about stopping. However, like everything in life, we need balance and knowing when and how to stop is one of the most important aspects of stress management. One of the key things I noticed when I left London and moved to a small, country town in Asia, many miles off the tourist track, was the difference in speed. In London it seemed to me that everything was done fast and with urgency. I used to think this was the only way to do things and that anytime I sat down and stopped, I was being lazy. My diary was not only filled during the week but also each weekend as in the reality that I had created, Friday and Saturday nights were made for 'socialising', to make up for the stress that I endured in the office. It's no wonder I burnt out! I just couldn't sustain the frenetic level of activity when I didn't allow myself time to stop.

When I lived in Asia, I suddenly found myself in a world where things were so much slower: there weren't distractions because as a foreigner, I couldn't understand the TV or newspapers. When it got dark, activities stopped and when it got light, activities started. And while it took a little while to get used to, once I had slowed down, life became so much richer. Rather than racing through each day, I actually noticed my environment, saw nature changing and had time to connect with people as well as myself. I had so much more creativity and excitement than I had ever felt before. Rather than feeling that I was in survival mode, I actually began to thrive.

While it is easy to assume that this was only possible because I was in a different country, the choice to slow down is open to all of us if we choose it. Stopping can so often be seen as a luxury in our society. Whereas our ancestors would have had highly active days followed by low activity nights and days, we tend to expect the same level of activity all the time. As part of my work as a massage therapist, I can often see the wrestle in my clients as they initially see having a massage as a 'treat' – that an hour to switch off is an indulgence rather than essential maintenance to stay healthy and well. However if we go back to the stress cycle in Chapter One, the fourth and final phase is 'Rest'. This final part of the stress cycle, which is so often ignored, is critical if we wish to maintain natural wellbeing and keep our stress levels in check.

I used to struggle with the concept of stopping as I had a strongly ingrained belief that unless I was 'out there', going at 100 mph, I was missing out. It was only when I became sick and was forced to stop – when my body had said enough is enough – that I started to appreciate the crucial importance of rest.

"For many years I burnt the candle at both ends and this was especially true when I was living in Singapore setting up two businesses. I had created a high paced, frenetic lifestyle where work was my sole priority. I thought nothing of sending work emails at 3.00am and then being back at my desk for 6.00am. My flat felt empty as I was either traveling across Asia seeing clients or partying hard with friends when I returned from business trips. Even when I started to feel unwell, I chose to ignore the growing feelings of fatigue and exhaustion and continued to drive myself, believing it was all down to me. It was only when I was about to launch a week-long training programme that I couldn't ignore my body anymore. While I struggled through the first day, I was unable to get out of bed on the second one. This was the beginning of a long road to recovery. My extreme living needed an extreme recovery.

It was during the three months that I spent on a farm, mainly sleeping, that I finally understood the cost of my relentless lifestyle."

— Danielle, *Coach*

To understand why this is, we need to have a simple overview of the nervous system that controls both the voluntary and the autonomic behaviour of our body. While this may sound a little complicated, it actually very simple as all we need to remember is that activities that come under the 'voluntary' system are actions that we intentionally (or voluntarily) do, such as making a cup of tea, drinking a large glass of wine or walking up the stairs. Actions that come under the autonomic system happen subconsciously (automatically) in so much that we don't consciously do anything to make them happen. An example of this would be when we sweat, breathe, blush or go into the stress response.

Now (stay with me reader) the autonomic nervous is divided into two parts – the stressed part and the not stressed part. The more scientific among us would call this the sympathetic nervous system (fight or flight) and the parasympathetic nervous system (rest and repair). While both parts are of equal importance, they have very different functions and can't work at the same time.

Imagine two identical twins: one twin embodies the sympathetic qualities. He is responsible for fight or flight and ensuring survival. He encompasses all symptoms relating to the stress response. His whole body pulsates with adrenaline and cortisol, his muscles are tense and his body is wired as his increased heart rate and blood pressure ensure that all his energy is ready for attack or defense. The other twin embodies the parasympathetic state and his job is to create the calm after the storm of the stress response. He carries out vital repair and rebalancing work that is needed after the stress hormones have been rampaging through the blood stream. Examples of his work would include normalising digestion and the sexual response, lowering blood pressure as well as reducing stress hormones.

As both of these states come under the autonomic nervous system, they happen outside of our conscious control and are actioned through different triggers. So while the sympathetic twin comes alive through triggers such as fear, stimulants, dehydration and refined sugars, the parasympathetic twin is activated by much slower activities such as focused breathing, soothing touch, essential oils, water, sleep and darkness.

When we rush from one stress trigger to another and don't stop, the parasympathetic twin is denied his life's calling. This puts a massive strain on the sympathetic twin as he is working double or triple shifts and using up all his reserves in the process. Our sleep, digestion, sexual desires and energy levels are all depleted and if this is not rectified then ultimately this leaves us burnt out – a state that involves an enforced stop and often, bed rest. Getting rebalanced after being burnt out is a challenging task and in many cases, for us to regain our natural wellbeing and 'mojo', we'll need to make significant lifestyle changes.

I used to find it very frustrating that after working hard for a long period of time, as soon as I had a holiday, I became unwell.

Now most of us have very busy lives inside and outside of the office. Being told to stop and slow down can initially seem impossible: just seem to be another thing to put on the ever-expanding 'To-Do' list. However, unless we see that our whole health and happiness depends on this then rather than choose to have time out, our body will enforce it upon us through ill health. I used to find it very frustrating that after working hard for a long period of time, as soon as I had a holiday or a day off, I became unwell. It could be anything from a cold or flu to a migraine. Suddenly the time off that I had been looking forward to was ruined, as I'd either carry on with my plans, feeling rotten in the process, or surrender to my bed.

> "When I worked in London it was of considerable concern that when I went on holiday I regularly suffered a severe migraine. It would normally occur on the second day just when I had started to relax and enjoy time with the family. It would become necessary for me to lie down in a dark room feeling pain and sickness for a number of hours, and I would then feel washed out on recovery."
> — Nigel, *Surveyor*

If you've been overdoing it for long periods of time, you may notice that you become sick once you stop. This concept, described as 'leisure sickness', was first described by Dutch psychologists Ad Vingerhoets and Maaike van Huijgevoort who found that people with high pressure jobs or who had been working on long and challenging problems at work, suffered from illness once the pressure was taken off and they stopped. Typically, the ailments most common to leisure sickness are headaches, migraines, fatigue and muscular aches and pains.

The reason for this is that when we are fuelled by adrenaline, this will override our body's natural responses and although it depletes our immune system, we initially won't feel tired and run down. It is only when we finally allow ourselves to stop that our body seizes this chance to detox and get rid of the stress hormones that have been building up over time. While many of us enjoy the 'high' and initial buzz of challenging problems, we can't allow work to take priority over our health. Putting oneself first takes discipline, but unless we do then ultimately our productivity will suffer as will the quality of our work.

So What Is Stopping Like?

It's all very easy to talk about stopping and pausing but how does 'stopping' manifest in our every day lives? Well like everything, it's different for each of us, depending on our lifestyles and personality type. While this is an incredibly broad generalisation, we tend to be fall into two personality types: extroverts or introverts. Extroverts usually recharge their batteries by being around other people and participating in social activities, while our extrovert friends can spend time on their own, this wouldn't rebalance them in the same way that it would for an introvert. The introverts among us recharge their batteries by having time out, away from other people and social activities. That's not to say they aren't social creatures, they just often need time alone to recharge their batteries and feel balanced.

> "Both my husband and I need short bursts of time alone to stay balanced. When my husband comes back from a busy day at work, the best thing I can do is actually leave the house for half an hour. This gives him the space to unwind and change head space from property developer to husband and father."
> — Susannah, *Health Professional*

Ultimately the best way to trigger the parasympathetic system will be different for each of us, however the most important thing is to find a way to stop and slow down that feels comfortable and realistic so that it can be sustained in the long term. The different ways of 'stopping' were first written about by an American cardiologist Herbert Benson in the 1970s. He used the phrase "The Relaxation Response" and saw, through his work, the importance of regularly allowing the body to enter this state of being. The Relaxation Response requires four components: a quiet environment, repetition of a sound, word, phrase or movement, a passive attitude and a comfortable position. This simple style of meditation was revolutionary forty years ago when Benson first brought forward the idea that relaxation could lower blood pressure and de-stress the mind and body. We now have a huge amount of choice when it comes to triggering the parasympathetic system and many of these techniques can be used within the workplace.

Calm Breathing

"Practicing regular, mindful breathing can be calming and energising and can even help with stress-related health problems from panic attacks to digestive disorders."
— Andrew Weil M.D. Founder, professor and director of the Arizona Center for Integrated Medicine

I always believe in keeping it simple. One of the best pieces of advice that I was given was to spend ten minutes each day doing nothing except breathing slowly and rhythmically. Breath seems to feature a lot in this book, the reason being that this is one of the most effective stress reducing techniques, as when we're consciously breathing, it stops adrenaline being released in our body taking it quickly out of fight or flight mode.

When I first tried to 'do nothing' for ten minutes, (this was before I spent a month in silent meditation, but I'll save that for another book!) my mind was really active and tasks kept popping my head. I wanted to get up and 'get going' as my mind said I had too much to do and that sitting breathing for ten minutes was a complete waste of time. However, when I persevered I could feel each part of my body unwind and rather than having to 'think about' slowing my breathing down, it started to naturally slow down. Instead of thinking about all the tasks that I should have been doing, ideas and creative thoughts flashed into my head that would help to make my life easier. When my ten minutes were up, I started work from a completely different space. Rather than feeling rushed and impatient, I was calm and grounded and my work was of a much better quality.

Anytime you notice that you are rushing around (clue: shallow breathing), taking ten minutes to stop will dramatically increase your productivity.

Breath-counting

This is a very simple and effective short meditation, often used in the Zen practice, to calm and refocus our 'monkey mind'. This is ideal to use any time that you feel yourself entering the fight or flight zone and want to stay grounded and present.

Sit in a comfortable position with the spine straight and head inclined slightly forward. Gently close your eyes and take a few deep breaths. Let your breath come naturally without trying to influence it. You may notice that your mind becomes very chatty and has a lot to say. This is fine – just observe the mind and focus on the numbers.

- To begin the exercise, count "one" to yourself as you exhale.

- The next time you exhale, count "two," and so on up to "five."

- Then begin a new cycle, counting "one" on the next exhalation.

Sensory Smells

The parasympathetic system is very much triggered by smells and using different essential oils in the office is really beneficial. There are lots of different ways you can do this although I would advise that you avoid the candle diffusers as they are likely to set off the fire alarm! I think the simplest way is either putting some essential oils drops directly onto a tissue and inhaling regularly or creating your own essential oil air spray. This requires a spray bottle (preferably glass), filling it with water, adding several drops of essential oil, shaking the bottle and then giving it a good spray around you.

While there are many essential oils available, my favourite oils for the office are lavender, frankincense and rosemary. As you may be in close proximity to your colleagues, you do need to bear in mind that we all react differently and while you may love a particular smell, others may have the opposite reaction! So ask them first before you use any oils in a shared space, and if there is any opposition to this, then use oils on a handkerchief instead.

Lavender: an excellent calming oil and ideal if your office is a stress hub. It's great for releasing tension headaches and calming your central nervous system if you're feeling restless and not able to concentrate.

Frankincense: is ideal if you have a racing mind and are finding it difficult to focus on one task. It encourages deeper breathing and helps to prioritise when there is a lot going on.

Rosemary: helps sharpens the mind, especially good for a Monday morning or a post lunch afternoon pick me up.

Foods That Stress

What we eat has a massive impact on the autonomic nervous system. There are many foods that can trigger us into fight or flight mode and while these include most processed foods that contain refined sugars; teas, coffee, alcohol and meat are also affect the autonomic system. While we need to monitor the labels and avoid any ingredients that we can't pronounce, it is also important to remember that *how* the food was grown and harvested impacts our stress response. The quality of our food is quite different to how it was 30 years ago. The change in farming practices and increased use of pesticides means that we're ingesting many more chemicals than our predecessors, which creates stress within the body.

> "Pesticides, by their very nature, are designed to kill living organisms, so it is not surprising that these chemicals are highly poisonous substances. Many people have suffered and reported ill-health effects following exposure to these chemicals. Pesticides have been strongly linked to many illnesses and diseases, including various cancers, Parkinson's disease, MS, MND, ME, asthma, allergies and MCS, amongst others."
> — Georgina Downs, UK Pesticides Campaign, *The Observer*, 13th April 2003

When I lived in India I stopped eating meat, however when camping in the Himalayas, the guide bought a sheep from the local shepherd which was cooked on the camp fire and eaten that evening. I was hungry, and there was little else to eat, so I joined in, but later that evening and the next day, felt incredibly tense and anxious. I also had very vivid dreams about being killed! As the change in my stress levels was so dramatic and fast, I looked into what the stress trigger was. I believe that although the meat was healthy and 'free range', my stress response was due to having eaten the stress hormones that the lamb had released before it had been killed. Like humans, animals release adrenaline and cortisol when they are experiencing stress and fear and this stays within the meat after they are killed. When I lived in London, meat was a regular part of my diet and I'm sure that I reacted this way often without realising it. It was only by being away from my usual distractions that I was able to notice how different choices triggered my stress response.

> "The British are paying a high price for the 'cheap' chicken and mince and dubiously economical sausages they've demanded in recent years. An animal terrified and traumatised as it is pitched towards death in the abattoir will understandably go into some sort of muscular spasm and the subsequent toughness of meat reflects this. And a little later on in the food chain that tough meat is tenderised by any number of additives in bottles of muck, for the domestic kitchen and in pre-prepared supermarket meals, which are not called junk food for nothing."
> — Jack Temple, *Medicine Man*

Foods That De-stress

> 'We call have up to 100 trillion cells in our bodies, each one demanding a constant supply of daily nutrients in order to function optimally. Food affects all of those cells, and by extension every aspect of our being: mood, energy levels, food cravings, thinking capacity, sex drive, sleeping habits and general health. In short, healthy eating is the key to wellbeing.''
> — Dr Gillian McKeith, *You Are What You Eat*

So while there foods that wake up the sympathetic twin, there are also foods that strengthen our parasympathetic twin. Charlotte Watts and Anna Magee in *The De-stress Diet* state that celery is one of the best foods for de-stressing the body as just four stalks a day actively lowers blood pressure as the chemicals apigenin and phthalide expand the blood vessels and activate the parasympathetic system.

Almonds are also great for de-stressing as they contain high levels of magnesium, which supports adrenal function. It is even better if these can be soaked overnight as it helps with digestion. Oats (again soaked overnight) are a great tonic for the nervous system as they are very nourishing and help to rebalance symptoms of exhaustion and anxiety.

I recommend delving into *The De-Stress Diet* as it is enlightening to see how you can alleviate stress symptoms by looking at your food choices.

Touch

Touch is one of the most powerful ways we can nurture the parasympathetic system. Since we were babies, touch has been our first language and how we were able to connect with others. There is something so nurturing about positive touch that I see it as one of the most effective forms of stress release. Having given and received regular massage for many years, I can see the huge changes that it can bring about in a small amount of time. As well as being deeply relaxing, it brings us out of our heads and back into our bodies. When we're functioning from the neck upwards, we're often over-analysing. However when we are connected to the whole of our body, we are in touch with our heart, which is where I believe our innate wisdom resides.

"As an osteopath, I'm still amazed that touch isn't honored more in our society. As our first sense, touch is a sacred communication and it's the deepest connection that we can have. Even in our fast-paced and often disconnected world, each one of us can easily access the benefits of touch to bring us back into reality and our greater selves. And it's so beautifully simple – a hug or gentle hand-hold is one of the most effective ways of dissolving tension. Even if you are on your own, you can create a 'touch' ritual for self-massage – using aromatherapy oils and soothing music. Staying connected in this way is a great gift to ourselves."
— Avni Trivedi, Founder of Touch. www.avni-touch.com

Music

Different styles of music can hugely affect our moods and state of being. As a massage therapist, one of my delights is finding appropriate music to accompany each treatment. With Spotify and YouTube being so accessible, experiencing different styles of music has never been so easy. Having a playlist ready for times of 'pausing' is a wonderful thing we can do for ourselves. Lighting a candle and pressing 'play' can transport us out of the reptilian, stressed mentality into an oasis of calm. One of my favourite pieces of music is by Arvo Part, an Estonian composer who created many albums including Alina. It has been described as "the tears of ghosts," which I think sums up this beautiful yet haunting music really well. I played this recently for a client one evening. My treatment room was only lit with candles and when the music started, you could also hear the wind outside. The stillness in the room was so powerful and due largely to the presence of this deeply healing music.

Remembering The Bigger Picture

Magical things happen when we slow down.

One of the reasons that we don't allow ourselves to stop is the mistaken belief that we are too busy and that we can only slow down when a certain task or challenge is overcome. As we discussed in the previous chapter, we'll never get to the bottom of our 'To-Do' list and it is more effective to schedule short stops into our daily lives than one long break a few times a year. We're all busy and unless we are top surgeons (and even then I would argue that I'd prefer to be treated by a doctor who was adequately rested rather than be at the mercy of his sympathetic side), we really CAN allow ourselves to take time to slow down and pause. Yes it may mean delegating or asking for help but the world will carry on turning with or without us.

Time Away

Having time away from your usual routine is a wonderful way to stop and pause. While I used to have several weeks off in one go, I now find myself taking shorter breaks which seem to work better for me as just three days in a different environment, recharges my batteries and gives me time to stop and reflect on the direction that my life is following.

"Not often, but occasionally I reach the point where I just have to stop, and it happens more as I get older. The problem is that often I can't stop, not even for a day, and if I'm not careful I end up in a vicious circle: there are things I have to do when I would like to be doing something else because I'm exhausted, but I've got to keep going and so become yet more tired and hungry for a break. That's when life starts to get less satisfying. For me that's why holidays are so important. Now I take holidays regularly and I really look forward to them. The pause in routine is so precious."
— Karren Brady, *Strong Woman*

Earlier this year I spent a weekend on a retreat called 'The Pause' which was run by Danielle Marchant, the Founder of Enabling Evolution. While there were many wonderful activities, the feedback from the attendees was that one of the best things was having unscripted time to do 'nothing'. As Danielle always say, "magical things happen when we slow down".

Agape Cottage is a truly magical sanctuary run by Sharon Agates. This cottage nestled in Great Warley in Essex exudes love and care and is the ultimate place to stop and rest. www.agapecottage.co.uk

One of the best things we can do when we need to stop is to leave work on time, cancel any plans and turn off our phone. Having quality time with ourselves to rest and relax is one of the most important things we can do to help stay balanced and stress-free.

Visulisation Exercise

- Close your eyes and take three deep breaths:

- Imagine a speedometer in front of you – notice how fast your day-to-day speed is.

- Imagine yourself in an environment where you feel comfortable to stop and rest. Slow down your speedometer to a speed that enables your parasympathetic system to take over. This is your own personal speed, which allows important repair work to happen within your body.

- Make a note of that speed.

- When you are resting, mentally set your internal speedometer to your parasympathetic speed.

Natural Law No. 8

Sleep

> "Sleep is God – go worship!"
> — Jim Butcher, *Death Masks*

Getting a good night's sleep is key for our natural wellbeing. It's when we sleep that our parasympathetic system, which does all of the important maintenance and repair work, is at its height. Sleep gives our body a natural reboot, recharging all of our biological systems as well as allowing our mind to off-load any worries or tensions that it has accumulated during the day. When we are well rested we have increased productivity, a better memory and more creativity. When we can't sleep, or aren't getting enough, then our immune system becomes depleted, our thinking is less clear and we feel tired, irritable and less motivated about life. Going to work when we haven't slept well is hard. Small annoyances and obstacles can easily spiral out of all proportion as being tired makes us more vulnerable to stress triggers and feeling overwhelmed.

> "Going to work when I am tired is like swimming in treacle. It all seems much harder and I'm much more sensitive to imagined slights. Innocent comments can easily get misconstrued inside my sleep deprived mind."
> — Carey, *Community Warden*

When we're worried about work, then it can very quickly affect our sleep. If it's a short-term issue such as a presentation or meeting then it is unlikely to do any longer term harm as we can often 'catch up' on our sleep debt the next night. However, unresolved ongoing worries about finances, redundancy or the job itself are something that we want to avoid at all costs. The reason for this is that without sleep we simply can't function at our optimum. Sleep deprivation has been used as a torture device for centuries and the results show that very quickly, the person deprived of sleep and rest becomes confused, disorientated and open to hallucinations. Neuroscientist Russell Foster says that when people are sleep-deprived, they act much more recklessly, especially men. As decisions are less considered, mistakes are more common. When we're not sleeping properly then we're not releasing the stress hormones that are building-up, so we tend to crave stimulates especially sugar and caffeine, which create more stress in the body. Perhaps it is no surprise that after oil, coffee is the highest trading index on the stock markets.

> "Almost everyone, including our world leaders and governments are keeping going on coffee and tea. I wonder about this: does it mean they are really in a state of constant sympathetic arousal? In which case, it is no surprise that decisions seem to be made that are totally about reacting in the present, rather than considering the impact of current action on future generations."
> — Pip Waller, *Holistic Anatomy*

In scientific investigations carried out in 1894, the Russian scientist Marie de Manaceine experimented with sleep deprivation on dogs and found that puppies will die within 10 days when deprived of sleep; more recent experiments in the 1980s showed similar results when pairs of rats were subjected to total sleep deprivation: they died after between 11 and 32 days of sleep deprivation – much earlier than the rats which were deprived of food. Although the specific cause of death in both cases are unknown, the link between lack of sleep and death was established as conclusive.

Another reason why sleep is vital is that it allows our subconscious mind to resolve issues that arise during the day. My father has always been a great advocate of 'sleeping on the problem' and I'm often amazed at how a solution can become apparent after

I have allowed myself to sleep on it. Apparently Napoleon also subscribed to this theory as historians have claimed that before he went to sleep he would imagine a cabinet with multiple drawers in it. He would place all his current problems inside the drawers, shut it tight and then sleep – fully expecting to have solutions upon waking.

When we're sleeping well, we can often take it for granted, however when we're stressed or worried, the quantity and quality of sleep is often effected. For some people this can manifest as problems falling asleep and for others it can be problems staying asleep as they can find themselves waking up at three or four in the morning with a racing, overactive mind. The most common reason for this is that the mind is unable to switch off as the stress hormones adrenaline and cortisol are creating that wired, wide-awake feeling, overriding the calm, wind-down feelings that we require for good quality sleep.

If we've been having problems getting to sleep for more than a few days, then it can be very easy to panic (which in itself becomes a vicious cycle). However the most important thing is to stay calm as in many cases we need less sleep than we think. Whereas eight hours is often given as the norm, many cultures, tribes and individuals survive on less. Daniel Browne in *The Energy Equation* cites many examples of different cultures that do not follow the eight-hour rule. The Masai tribe in Africa sleeps three to four hours a night and Margaret Thatcher is famous as someone who only slept five hours each night. The whole concept of having eight hours of consecutive sleep is relatively new to our society and was born out of the Industrial Revolution when workers needed more structured time for their shift work. Before this, people would often sleep in blocks of time – fours hours with a two-hour waking period followed by another four hours. The two-hour waking time in between sleep was often used for reading, procreating, or even for analysing the dreams that they had just experienced. Some scientists believe that people who regularly wake in the middle of the night are actually more in tune with their ancestors' sleeping patterns.

However, unlike our ancestors who had more time available to rest, we need to make the most of the hours we have to source good quality sleep so that we feel refreshed and can enjoy our 'awake' hours. For this, we need to look at our lifestyle behaviour patterns, as these are the key to the harnessing of a good night's sleep.

Firstly, our diet impacts the quality of our sleep as the foods that we eat and the liquids we consume can have a big impact on our nocturnal patterns. And the number one culprit for sleep irregularities is caffeine.

Caffeine

Caffeine is actually a poison as in its natural state it contains pesticide qualities in its seeds, leaves and fruits which can paralyse and kill certain insects that feed off it. It has been used for centuries as a 'pick me up' and one of the first recorded usages was in the ninth century when an Ethiopian shepherd noticed his goats were "elated" and unable to sleep after grazing on caffeine cherries. When we consume caffeine in our drinks, food and medication (check the labels!), it stimulates the nervous system to create the fight or flight response by releasing huge amounts of adrenaline directly into the bloodstream. So while we do get a boost of energy, it's only illusionary as the adrenaline and subsequent stress response just masks the underlying tiredness. While a caffeine rush peaks within 30 to 60 minutes, it stays within the bloodstream for around five hours – more if caffeine content is high – keeping us in that stressed and anxious state associated with the sympathetic system. For us to get the best quality sleep, we really need to avoid caffeine in the afternoon and especially the evenings. Substances with high levels of caffeine in include: teas, coffees, energy drinks artificial sweeteners, medication.

Alcohol

While many people rely on alcohol to drop-off to sleep, it actually confuses our natural sleep pattern and rather than awake refreshed, we're more likely to feel groggy, tired and stressed in the morning. The reason for this is that our sleep pattern is divided into four stages. Stage one and two are the lighter sleep stages which we awake from easily as we remain aware of our environment during this the time. The third and final stages of sleep are the much heavier stages where our body does its core recharge work. The last stage is known as REM (rapid eye movement) and this is where we dream. As we tend to go through all the stages between three and five times each night, all of us, when we have a good night's sleep, will dream whether or not we remember any of them in the morning. There are many physiological theories based on dreams that show that they are a critical part of brain function as they exercise various neural pathways that are connected to how we absorb and take in new information. There are also many psychological theories which state that dreams allow our subconscious mind to de-stress as this is how the body sorts through and resolves problems and issues that arise during the day. However when we drink alcohol it lightens our sleep cycle and suppresses that all-important REM stage. While people who have been drinking alcohol often find it easier to fall asleep, they will often awake regularly throughout the night, as the alcohol works through their system which deprives them of passing into the heavier, latter stages of sleep.

Sleeping Patterns

For many of us, when we have a heavy meal late in the evening, we'll often notice that this affects the quality of our sleep. Whereas it makes sense that consuming large quantities of food is not conducive to sleeping (because our body is actively digesting), Chinese medicine explains simply that our body has a natural cycle, which when followed, allows us optimum health and sleep. This Five Element system, which has been based on observations of human behaviour for thousands of years, breaks down our body's functions into 24-hour periods. The wheel shows that our organs naturally have periods of heightened, peak activity in two-hour intervals, followed by periods of relative rest. If we are able to work with our organs in their peak times, we're putting less stress on ourselves and we'll be more in the flow. An example of this is that between seven and nine in the morning, our stomach system is most active; this makes it a good time for having breakfast (ideally the biggest meal of the day) as our digestion will be at its optimum. After nine am, the stomach enters it's rest period, so having large amounts of food between nine and eleven am will, in many instances make us feel bloated, tired and less energised as any food will be harder for our body to digest.

If we awake during the night, it can be useful to see what organ is at its peak as this can highlight any areas that are out of balance. As the liver is at its most active between 1 and 3am, any lifestyle overload will often mean that we awake during this time. This is because our liver is our main detoxification centre, so if we've been stressed, taking medication, alcohol or toxins then this will mean that our liver has to work extra hard. As the Chinese connect the liver with feelings of anger, if we have been feeling angry towards someone or something, then this will also impact our sleep as the liver will also be breaking down these emotions during this time.

While there are many books and resources that expand upon this in great detail I recommend the book *Traditional Acupuncture: The Law of the Five Elements* by Dr Dianne M Connelly. (The website link www.astrodreamadvisor.com/Qi-Cycle.html has a simple but informative overview of the different organ cycles.

Sleeping Pills

While sleeping pills look like an effective quick fix, they are never a good idea for a number of reasons. Firstly they are masking the problem and/or the lifestyle behaviour that is causing the sleep problem. There is a reason why our sleep is being compromised and unless we look more deeply to try and understand what this is, then the problem will remain. The second reason is that sleeping pills are highly psychologically addictive. People taking them can very quickly start to rely on them as their means of getting to sleep.

In my last year at University, I shared a noisy house and as my bedroom was next to the front door, I was often woken by people coming in late or leaving early. I decided that if I took some sleeping pills then I would sleep through these disruptions and thus be more awake in the morning. However while my sleeping pills, bought in the local supermarket, did knock me out each evening, I woke feeling very groggy and it took me hours to wake up properly. Although I didn't feel any more awake in the morning (in reality I actually felt worse), before I knew it I became reliant on taking them, thinking that this was my only route to sleep. It was only when I had a lifestyle change and moved bedrooms that I felt secure enough to stop taking them.

Watching TV

Another reason for sleep problems is watching TV before we go to bed – or even, in bed. Our brain cannot distinguish between what is real and what is false so if we are watching a gripping film or even the news, we'll experience the same rollercoaster of emotions as if we were really there, either in the film or any areas of problems that the news is reporting upon. Ironically, one of the easiest habits to get into is falling asleep on the sofa if you're watching TV in the evenings. Not only does this affect your posture (you're more likely to have shoulder and neck problems if you do this regularly) but the mind has to process the visual imagery and associated emotions that it gets from the TV. You'll have a much better quality sleep if you are disciplined enough to turn the TV off (setting an alarm can work well otherwise it's easy to get sucked into TV land) and go to bed earlier in the evening as it allows the mind and body to wind down. The same thing happens if we are on the Internet and then immediately try to go to sleep: not only is the bright glare from the screen contradictory to the dark that our minds need to enter the parasympathetic state, but again, our bodies have to spend time de-charging all the visual stimulus that it gets from the computer.

Creating A Night-time Ritual

Babies and children sleep better when a night-time ritual is in place, and so too do adults. Having at least twenty to thirty minutes to wind-down hugely enhances the quality of our sleep and we'll feel more awake and recharged in the morning. While each of us has different preferences, ideally our sleep ritual would follow a similar pattern each evening so that we can start associating the activities with slowing down and going to sleep. As we are entering the parasympathetic state, the first thing we want to do is eliminate loud, intrusive noises and bright lights. Soft lighting makes a huge difference to our mental state. Having a bath or warm shower is also ideal as symbolically we're washing off the day preparing ourselves for rest. Lavender essential oil is also renowned for being a sedative and inducing sleep – you can either put six drops directly into the bathwater or put it on your pillow or a tissue in the bedroom. The night-time ritual is also an ideal time for clearing the mind and writing down anything that needs to be done the next day so that your mind doesn't need to hold on to anything. Having a piece of paper or a journal by the bed is ideal for this.

Power Naps

If you've had a disturbed night's sleep or can feel your energy waning during the day then power naps can be very useful. I find that power naps are often derided and the reason for this is that they are used incorrectly. To make the most of a power nap you need to make sure that you don't pass the first or second stage of sleep, which means that you shouldn't nap for more than 30 minutes during the day. The first two stages are the lighter stages and are ideal for recharging and giving us that quick boost if we feel our energies waning. After thirty minutes we can return to our desk, more recharged and motivated from the power nap. However if we nap for longer (or past 4pm) then we risk entering the third stage of sleep, which is a much heavier stage and typically rather than feeling recharged, we'll feel tired, cold, disorientated and will want to sleep for longer.

People in Spain and other Mediterranean countries have been taking a daily power nap for centuries – and it is known as a 'siesta'. Ancient folklore suggests that when taking a siesta, you should recline on the chaise holding a heavy door key in your hand. When you are about to fall from stage two sleep into deeper sleep, you will let go of the key, and its clattering to the floor will wake you up, refreshed and ready for the remains of the day!

The Feet

A technique that is used in the East for sleeping problems, especially when you have a lot on your mind is putting your feet in a cold bath. A variation on this is wearing socks that have been in the freezer (although I have yet to try this). The logic behind this is that the energy – or as they would say in the East – the *chi* – is moved away from the mind and directed to the feet. This stops us focusing on worries or upcoming tasks as the body is focused on warming-up the feet. While it may sound a little strange, its incredibly effective and I'd recommend this practice if you notice that your mind is racing when you're trying to get to sleep.

As a reflexologist, I find that treatments on the feet are great at helping rebalance sleeping patterns. As well as being incredibly relaxing, any work on the feet helps to ground us and allow us to come out of our heads and back into our bodies. Whenever I've been doing a lot of 'head work' such as writing, driving or using the computer, I always make sure I rebalance by focusing on the feet, even just walking bare foot in the garden for five minutes allows me to feel grounded and present again.

When I see clients with sleep problems I always make sure their treatment includes work on the pineal gland; a gland that is found in the brain that releases melatonin and is responsible for maintaining our sleeping patterns. There is a reflexology point in the big toe (and thumb) that relates directly to this gland and even gentle self-massage around this area can hugely help relax the body and help with sleep.

Valerian

Valerian, once referred to as the 'Valium of the 19th Century', is a natural remedy that has been used for centuries to help with insomnia and sleeplessness. It is available in tablets, capsules and teas and while some people may not notice a difference for two to three weeks, this remedy is an excellent relaxant for getting to sleep. As its natural aroma can be a little off-putting (some people say it reminds them of smelly socks), many people prefer the capsule format to the tea. It should not be used in the long term (for more than six months), or with alcohol or during pregnancy or breastfeeding.

Viridian, www.viridian-nutrition.com is one of my favourite vitamin suppliers. I love their ethos and their products are all of an excellent standard. They sell valerian root in capsules and as a tincture.

Herbal Teas

Chamomile is an excellent tea to have in the evenings as it helps the body to naturally unwind and enter the parasympathetic stage. I tend to have chamomile tea when I've had a busy day and notice that, rather than naturally winding down, as the evening advances I'm getting more and more fired up and restless. Having a cup of chamomile tea really helps me settle and allows my body to calm itself down. Like anything, do read the labels as some chamomile teas contain caffeine which is obviously something we want to avoid.

I'm a great fan of the Pukka range of teas which are all organic and ethically sourced. As well as doing a lovely golden chamomile blend (caffeine free), they do a night-time range which is very effective and tastes delicious. The ingredients include oat flower, chamomile flower, lavender flower and valerian root. www.pukkaherbs.com

Finally, while we all have different natural sleep patterns, if you notice that your sleeping has become irregular or changed significantly then it's always important to investigate why. Obviously if you have had a major life change such a new baby, new job or just moved house then this can explain why your sleep has become unsettled for a short period of time. However if there hasn't been a major life upheaval or you notice that your sleep has been disrupted for more than three weeks – this tends to be seen as the cut off stage between acute (short term) and chronic (long term) problems – then it is useful to seek outside support. Depending on your preference this could be your local GP or a holistic practitioner such as a homeopath, yoga instructor, counsellor or massage therapist/reflexologist.

Visualisation Exercise

- Close your eyes and take three deep breaths:

- Imagine your own personal sleep tank – it can be any size or shape that you wish.

- Notice how much sleep you have in reserve.

- Decide how much sleep you wish to bank from now on in.

- Before you fall asleep mentally set your tank to be replenished to your desired amount.

Nature

Natural Law No. 9

Nature

"Look deep into nature, then you will understand everything better."
— Albert Einstein

When we work in an office all day it's easy to forget that we are part of nature. For many years I took very little notice of what was going on outside the window as firstly I couldn't actually see a window from my desk and secondly the air conditioning and heating maintained the same temperature whatever the time of the year. Sitting at my desk each day was like working in a microclimate as I could wear short sleeves T-shirts in the heart of winter and wool wraps in the summer when strangely the office was most cold. Consequently, my work and lifestyle pretty much ignored the different seasons and I expected to have the same level of health, energy and productivity regardless of the time of year.

However, whether we are aware of it or not, our bodies behave very differently depending on the season. We may feel a loss of energy during the winter months when getting out of bed can require immense discipline while in spring we can leap out of bed in minutes. The reason is that each season has a different focus and energetic quality which as well as effecting animals, plants and vegetables, also impacts us. Nature is a wonderful mirror of our own natural cycles and we only have to look outside to understand why we may be feeling a specific way or wanting to do certain activities.

"The best remedy for those who are afraid, lonely or unhappy is to go outside, somewhere where they can be quiet, alone with the heavens, nature and God. Because only then does one feel that all is as it should be and that God wishes to see people happy, amidst the simple beauty of nature".

— Anne Frank, *The Diary of a Young Girl*

While it may not be possible to design our work around the different seasons, just by understanding how we are affected during different times of the year can help maintain our natural wellbeing and reduce our stress levels.

The Seasons

Since I began to focus upon my own wellbeing and started to understand the true power of nature, I've always found it a little odd that the 1st January is regarded as THE day that heralds the beginning of the new year, as really there is nothing 'new' happening in nature – we're actually in the heart of winter and still very much in hibernation mode. Taking on any New Year resolutions at this time goes against our natural inclination, which isn't necessarily up for great changes. I've always believed that as spring is nature's New Year – as this is when everything starts happening again – it would really make sense for us to start our year here as well. Interestingly, the earliest recorded New Year festivities, which date back 4,000 years ago to ancient Babylon, took place in March on the first new moon after the spring equinox. The 1st January is a relatively 'recent' Roman custom introduced by Caesar to mark the beginning of the year as well as honour the Roman god of new beginnings - Janus.

Spring

The word equinox comes from the Latin word meaning 'equal night'; and the Spring Equinox which takes place on the 21st March is when the day and night are approximately equal. Officially acknowledged as the first day of spring this is a very powerful time in nature as there is a major energetic shift from winter and if we are aware of it, we can harness the new, fresh energy that this season offers.

This is a great time for new beginnings and for sowing new seeds. Many people find that new projects and goals, that may have been stagnating or struggling to take off in winter, naturally move forward in spring.

> We'll sleep better, eat better, communicate better and generally feel better once we invite nature into our lives.

Spring is also a very popular time to undertake a detox or fast, as our body, wanting to shake off the dross of winter, is ripe for cleansing. For many of us this can manifest as a cold, cough or flu as the body takes advantage of the increased light and energy to have a good clear-out. Rather than resent the illness and see it as something to slow us down, it's actually a great thing as it releases and clears toxicity and afterwards, if we have managed it well, we'll feel so much better. In actual fact, we all need two to three colds a year to keep our immune system at its peak.

However, I'm sure that like me, you have experienced times when you feel that you're picking up every germ that's going around the office. Rather than blame your contaminated colleagues, this is a clear signal from your body that you're run-down and need to take action to restore your reserves. Ultimately, the simply truth is that we can't *catch* a cold or any illness. We can only get sick if we have a depleted immune system in the first place. I've been guilty of blaming my colleagues over the years, especially a manager who I believed gave me a particularly nasty strain of flu one Christmas. However it's actually a false notion that cold and coughs are 'out there', waiting to invade at any given opportunity. This common belief comes from Louis Pasteur, the French scientist who based all his theories of disease on the concept that germs are caught from the atmosphere rather than being connected to the person's health and wellbeing. However on his deathbed he revoked his former work by stating that "the germ is nothing; the internal environment is everything", although current medical theory tends to ignore this and still follows his former thinking.

Henry Lindlahr in *Natural Therapeutics: Philosophy Vol. I* explains that groups of people falling sick at the same time is due to us having similar lifestyles, eating habits and thought patterns as those around us rather than any airborne diseases. It would seem that following a similar track to our fellow colleagues creates a similar immunity, which is why some groups of people fall ill and other groups of people stay healthy.

If you do notice that you get sick around the Equinox then it shows that your body is working with the natural laws (which although uncomfortable is a good thing!). The best way to treat an acute (short term) illness such as a cold is to rest for three days, eating very little and drinking lots and lots of water. Fresh air is important too, so open the windows, even if it's just for quick blast to refresh your room. The wise saying of "If you feed a cold, you'll be starving a fever" is very apt as you want to avoid heavy meals and keep to light broths that can keep you hydrated without creating more work for your body. During an acute illness, our body temperature increases as it is through inflammation that our bodies moves the toxicity on, so we're likely to feel hot during this time, which again is a good thing. Epsom salts in the bath is especially helpful during this time as it is very detoxifying. Within three days any acute illness, which has not been suppressed with medication or 'ignored' by doing usual work activity, should have passed leaving you with a boosted immune system.

One of the biggest mistakes that I used to make when I felt ill was to carry on regardless and go into work. For some reason, I used to feel guilty taking time off if I was sick, so I'd drag myself into the office to show everyone how committed I was and how seriously I took my job (and no doubt myself). Not only would I be feeling terrible and very sorry for myself but I wasn't very productive and without realising it, was just prolonging the sickness. Now, whenever I get an acute illness, I treat it very differently and allow my body three days to have a good physical spring clean. I reschedule my clients, drink lots of body temperature water and go to bed. I avoid any heavy foods and keep to liquids and soups as much as possible. On the second day I have my Epsom salts bath, do some dry skin brushing (see below) to keep the circulation moving and depending on the weather (I wouldn't advise this if it's raining, snowing or very cold) go outside for a walk to breathe in some fresh air. Rather than having the cold/flu lingering on for days or weeks, it passes much more quickly and I feel so much better at the end.

Dry Skin Brushing

I'm a big fan of dry skin brushing. While it works well if you're feeling under the weather, it is also very useful to incorporate as a daily or weekly practice to helps your body get rid of toxicity. I find it especially useful in the winter as the effect is similar to taking exercise and warms my whole body up by kick-starting my circulatory system. The reason for this is that our skin is the body's largest organ of elimination. Dry brushing removes the scurf layer (the uppermost layer) which holds toxicity and acidity. By brushing this layer away, it removes these unwanted impurities and at the same time creates movement in the lymphatic system. We want lots of movement in the lymphatic system as this system is responsible for eliminating toxins, waste products, bacteria, excess water and viruses. Lymph, unlike blood that is pumped by the heart, can only move when we move so if it stagnates, lymph gets heavy and sticky and we'll feel more toxic. We may also notice that lymph nodes (found in the neck, under the arms and groin) will swell and become tender.

To start you'll need a long handled skin brush designed specifically for this purpose (found in good health stores). Start with gentle but brisk strokes on top of the right foot and work your way up the entire right leg. The skin will redden but it should not hurt. Repeat on left foot and leg. Brush the front and then back torso (always using circular motions and moving towards the heart). Brush the right hand and work your way up the entire right arm up to the shoulder. Repeat on left side. Do not brush the head or face.

Summer

Summer officially starts on the 21st June which is also referred to as the Summer Solstice as its the longest day of light for the year. As this is nature's season of growth and maturation, we too (and any projects that we are working on) are also maturing so this is an excellent time for working hard and getting things done. The increased light means that we have more energy available and (although I don't advocate this!) if we are to burn the candle at both ends, this is the time to do it. We also need less sleep during this season (again, children are good barometers and often much more in tune with nature, so look to their changing seasonal sleeping habits).

Try and make the most of this additional time by being outside as much as possible. It's especially important to stay hydrated in the summer months. Elson M Haas in *Staying Healthy with the Seasons* talks about sun teas being very beneficial for our bodies during this time. As well as being hydrating, they provide us with a wonderful dose of natural goodness.

Solar or Lunar Tea

Place dry or fresh herbs in a clear glass jug and put it in the sunlight or moonlight for one or two days/nights. Place in the fridge until you are ready to drink it and when you are, pour boiled water into a pot with one or several of the herbs and let it steep for 20 minutes. I especially like having lemon peel solar tea ready for my clients after a treatment – it encapsulates the smell of summer and is so refreshing!

Examples of good leaf flowers and herbs for solar and lunar tea are:

- Peppermint leaf
- Hibiscus flowers
- Lemon grass
- Red clover flowers
- Chamomile flowers
- Any green herbs
- Rosemary
- Orange or lemon peel

While you can order herbs online or from many health food shops, Neal's Yard is one of my favourite places to buy them. I always enjoy visiting their Covent Garden store although all their herbs can be ordered online: www.nealsyardremedies.com/dried-herbs

Autumn

The Autumn Equinox, which takes place on 21st September carries us into the autumn season. Like spring, the Autumn Equinox is a very powerful and beneficial time to cleanse. If you do decide to have a detox, I would advise that you consider your programme in advance. Having done intensive detoxes in India and Thailand (not for the faint hearted!) I've also done more gently cleanses on my own which in some cases have been just as effective.

Sarra Moore the Founder of 'Fresh' runs workshops specifically on detoxes for the Spring and Autumn Equinoxes. She always states the importance of preparing yourself for any internal cleansing rather than racing into any form of detoxification. Lack of preparation can create unpleasant healing reactions and also make the process much harder emotionally as well as physically.

> "The Autumn Equinox is the perfect time to cleanse so that our bodies can shift toxicity and stay strong and healthy during the darker and colder months. From all my years as a healthy eating coach, I have found this time to be the most powerful for detoxification, however it's important to get it right. So often people throw themselves into a detox without adequate thought and planning and wonder why they feel dreadful during and afterwards. My specially designed Equinox detoxes work with each individual to help them cleanse at a level that is best for them."
> — Sarra Moore, Founder, Fresh – *www.fresh-nutrition.co.uk*

As autumn is the time for harvest, this is when we can reap the benefits of all the hard work that we have done in spring and summer. It's a harmonious time for finishing anything outstanding be that projects, DIY or even relationships. I often find that anything that has been hanging about on my 'To-Do' list takes on an urgency in autumn, unlike any other time of the year.

Winter

Winter officially begins on the 21st December on the Winter Solstice. If you look outside the window during this time then there is nothing happening and really this is how our body wants to be –hibernating, resting and staying warm. Our ancestors who didn't have had access to electricity and light would have spent most of winter inside, doing very little. I'm often amazed at how much I want to sleep during the winter months and when I allow myself to do this it really sets me up for spring when the surge of increased energy is palpable.

In many ways, as much as I enjoy Christmas, it's a shame that in the northern hemisphere we have our main party season in the heart of winter as late nights and all the associated festivities stress our bodies more than any other time. Try to stay in balance by consciously making more time to sleep and rest in between any parties and late nights!

The Lunar Cycle

One of my favourite aspects of nature is the Lunar Cycle and I find it fascinating how the moon affects not just myself but others around me. We all have different associations when we think of the moon. My husband associates it with a big chunk of cheese while I tend to think about the nursery rhyme character Aiken Drum or the typical clip of the wolf baying at the moon in the film 'American Werewolf in London'. However for this next section, it would most useful if we could clear away our current cultural lunar beliefs so that we can investigate the relevance that the moon has upon our own natural wellbeing.

To start with, we just need to remind ourselves that the moon (and to a lesser extent the sun) is responsible for all the movement connected to the ocean tides. As we are 70% water (see Chapter Two for a refresher!) we too cannot help but be affected by the moon's gravitational pull which has four different stages. An entire lunar cycle lasts approximately 28 days, which like the different seasons, have a different focus and energetic quality. Knowing what stage the moon is in, will help us to work more in the natural flow.

The New Moon

The new moon is when the sun's gravitational force is pulling the moon away from the earth, which releases huge amounts of negative ions into the atmosphere. Negative ions are molecules that have gained an electrical charge and are found in abundance around waterfalls, the sea or even after a thunderstorm. These ions increase the oxygen flow to our blood which has a very decongesting impact on us. We're likely to feel much more healthy around a new moon as our body is effortlessly cleansing, leaving us recharged and energised. This is a great time to start a health regime or give up an unhealthy habit: not only are we less likely to experience withdrawal symptoms but we'll naturally find 'letting go' easier on a new moon.

Waxing Moon

The new moon is followed by a waxing moon which lasts for about two weeks. This is when the moon is getting bigger and in many ways so are we. Because of this, it's a great time for absorption, so any vitamins or good healthy foods that we ingest at this time are doubly effective. It's also a great time for learning new information as we naturally hold on to information more effectively around this time. However as the body is in 'holding-on' mode, this can also work against us if we're consuming high stress foods or experiencing high levels of stress. I notice that my clothes can quickly feel tight during the time of a waxing moon so I'm careful to eat lighter foods and ensure that I do my dry skin brushing to avoid any physical (as well as emotional!) stagnation.

Full Moon

The full moon is perhaps the most well known stage of the lunar cycle and can often be used in horror movies to depict scenes where people are apt to lose control. Although it is unlikely we'll turn into werewolves, research has shown that people do behave differently during a full moon. The Sussex police found a rise in violent incidences during a full moon and in 1998, a three-month psychological study of 1,200 inmates at Armley Jail in Leeds discovered a rise in violent incidents during the days either side of a full moon. One friend who is an occupational therapist working in a psychiatric hospital said that they always scheduled more staff during a full moon as patients tended to be more restless and stressed. So while people's behaviours can change, understanding what is happening in our outside environment can significantly help alleviate any uncomfortable symptoms associated with a full moon.

While the sun is pulling the moon away from the earth in a new moon, the opposite happens in a full moon as the sun is pulling the moon towards the earth. This releases large amounts of positive ions which have the opposite effect to the negative ions. Rather than feel refreshed, we're likely to feel more congested as positive ions constrict the blood flow around our bodies. As there is less oxygen flowing to the brain, we're more likely to feel irrational, irritated and less able to concentrate. It also means that anything we consume will have a stronger impact on our system so if you drink alcohol you may feel it's impact faster and have a stronger hangover the next day.

If you do notice that you feel out of sorts, keep breathing deeply (you want to keep as much oxygen flowing around the body as possible). Exercise is also helpful too as it releases all those stress hormones, and finally, remember it's just one day and as the proverb says 'this too shall pass'.

Waning Moon

After a full moon we enter the waning period. The waning period is an excellent time for releasing and detoxing. Like the time of the waxing moon when the moon is getting bigger, during a waning period, the moon is getting smaller which means that the environment is ideal for cleansing and releasing unwanted toxicity. We can often eat more without putting on weight and any cleansing work that we do is doubly beneficial.

It can also be a calmer and easier time in the office as people are more forgiving during a waning period as any unintended slights are easily 'let go' of. It's also a good time to finish or complete on goals, projects or relationships.

Astrology

One of my favourite aspects of the lunar cycle is astrology. I'm not talking about the stars that you read in the newspapers, but our own birth charts and how the placements of different planets influences our lives, careers and wellbeing. As an astrologer for 24 years, Sally Kirkman knows the value of working with natural laws to tap into universal knowledge. Astrology at its simplest level is about cycles: the regular movement of the planets that mirror the seasons of nature and the major turning points in our lives. Knowing where the planets are can help us live in tune with the natural cycles and that stay in flow.

This is seen most clearly in the journey of the sun which takes one year to transit from the first sign Aries, marking the Spring Equinox, through to Pisces, the last sign of the zodiac. The sun spends approximately one month in each of the 12 signs and these correspond to the seasons in the northern hemisphere. For example, the sun in Aries in the spring is the time to sow seeds whilst the sun in Virgo in late August/September is the perfect period to reap what you've sown and coincides with the harvest season.

A similar rhythm applies to the shorter cycle of the moon, which takes approximately 28 days to complete one cycle of the zodiac, spending 2-3 days in each sign.

> "When the moon is in Aries which is in the 1st House of my natal chart, I often move through life at turbo speed, rapidly getting things done and ticking off my 'To-Do' list. When the moon is in Libra, I often have less energy because I'm actively giving more to others. Astrology is most useful as a timing tool, as we can use the regular motion of the planets to not only understand our own lives

Nature

better, but to plan accordingly. For example, when Jupiter is active, we're advised to take risks, be adventurous and play big. Whereas when Saturn dominates, we're better off taking life at a slow pace, conserving our energy and holding something back. Many people are turning to astrology because they're more receptive to a metaphysical view of life and want to feel that they're on the right path. In today's world, the ancient wisdom of astrology can be an incredibly useful navigational tool to keep us in step with the natural flow of life."

— Sally Kirkman, *www.sallykirkman.com*

While this is a relatively short overview of our Natural Laws, the most important thing is for each of us to notice how we are individually affected by nature. For this we need to get outside and be in it, to actively part of this amazing earth creation. It doesn't have to be a mammoth exercise: it could just be taking a walk at lunchtime or opening the window to stare at the moon and stars at night. Nature is our natural healer and there is so much wisdom available for us once we start noticing. Embercombe www.embercombe.co.uk is an amazing environment to experience the true power of nature. Led by the inspirational Mac, Embercombe runs courses throughout the year and has opportunities for volunteers to live in yurts and learn more about sustainability and the land.

While it can be harder in the UK to initially be outside as there is more cold weather, once we wrap up warmly and start moving, the temperature has little impact. We'll sleep better, eat better, communicate better and generally feel better once we invite nature into our lives.

Visualisation Exercise

- Close your eyes and take three deep breaths.

- Take yourself to a place in nature that calls to you – it can be a place that you have actually visited or just read about.

- Look at the sky. Embrace the space around you.

- Imagine a strong wind and allow yourself to feel the healing power of nature – refreshing and revitalizing each muscle, bone and cell.

- Listen for any sounds around you.

- Use this visulisation any time you have spent a long time at your desk and wish to feel refreshed.

Natural Law No. 10

Passion

> "We ask ourselves, 'Who am I to be brilliant, gorgeous, talented, fabulous?' Actually, who are you not to be?"
> — Marianne Williamson, *A Return to Love*

The last Law is for me in many respects the most important one of all. When we're struggling and going against the natural flow, it's often a clear sign that we're out of harmony with life and our own natural wellbeing. I learned the wisdom of this law the hard way as for many years my life felt like hard work. I used to have a preconceived idea of how my life should be, based mainly on comparing myself to others: when I wasn't measuring up to where I thought I should be, I felt frustrated and that on some level I had failed. And as I was surrounded, for many years, by highly ambitious colleagues who were often very focused on the next rung in the ladder, I too, became obsessed with my career and pushing for the next pay rise or promotion. Yet interestingly I had never taken time to consider what I really wanted: all my targets and goals came from comparisons with other people. For so long, I was working towards goals that belonged to other people – my manager, my father and even the media, as newspapers and magazines regularly outlined where someone at my age should statistically be for 'success and happiness'. So while my colleagues may have been totally in their flow when focusing on sales or promotions, when I took some time out I came to the hard realisation that my heart wasn't in the corporate world, and that this environment went against my natural flow. However, although I realised that I wanted to create something different with my life, I just didn't know what that was.

"I now know that I spent my working life in Human Resources, planning what the next stage of my career needed to look like and never what I wanted my life journey to be. Without realising, I had been chasing a career path that didn't actually tick the boxes for me personally. It was only when fate lent a hand and I found myself in a redundancy situation and 5 months pregnant with my second child, that I was able to make the transition from the safety of paid employment to creating a business that I am passionate about and find fulfilling on every level. Admittedly, It hasn't always been easy: it has required resilience, belief, courage and determination, but when life presents you with an opportunity, sometimes you just have to take a leap of faith, step out of the comfort zone, into the adventure zone and run with it."
— Leigh Howes, Founder, *The Sorbus Group*

Focusing On Your Passion

Moving abroad for several years was part of my journey towards wellbeing, as by having time out from my normal routine it really helped me to focus on what my passion actually was. On reflection, the signs had always been there: all my books were about natural wellbeing and health; I could happily spend hours researching and reading different viewpoints; I would regularly invest my money in different types of bodywork treatments and studying the body's physiology never felt like work - I relished it. However while I was fascinated by complimentary health and had already completed a year-long reflexology diploma, I hadn't quite twigged that I too could work within this field.

The awareness only became clear to me when I was in New Zealand walking alongside a beautiful lagoon. My vision wasn't a massive 'change the world' premonition but I realised that I wanted to create a thriving business through massage, reflexology and education that allowed people to completely de-stress mentally and physically. The more I thought about it, the more excited I felt, and while my mind came up with many limiting beliefs, I knew deep down that this was something that I couldn't ignore. Once I had this vision in place then the struggle in my life was greatly reduced as I was working towards my own goal rather than trying to create and live someone else's dream.

Whilst I undertook a major life change to connect with my passion, it certainly does not have to be as arduous or as difficult as I made it! Creating my business – The Orange Grove: Natural Wellbeing – was worth every (challenging) step to get there and I feel huge gratitude that my work is centered around something that I am truly interested in and passionate about. However, igniting your passion does not mean that you have to leave your current job or turn your life upside down, unless of course that is what you want. Just spending time and energy on something that fires you up will give your life greater meaning and a much deeper sense of satisfaction. Before I go on, you may argue that you're too busy to add another activity in the mix, but I would say that we can always make time for things that are important: we can get creative about our time, give up less important things, say no more – as really, doing something you love is one of the most important things that we can do in our lives.

Work towards your own goals rather than living someone else's dream.

Some of us instinctively know what our passion is, whilst others of us need gentle reminding of our own core values rather than following the interests of those closest to us. I was listening to a radio programme a while ago and one of the presenters was saying that the education system often focuses on what children are struggling with, putting all the attention and time on that, rather than focusing on what the child is good at and putting all the focus on that. I thought that was really interesting. We all have our own unique skills that can at times get lost underneath the things that we're not so good at. As a clue, anything that isn't hard or a struggle is often one of our key strengths. It can be very easy to negate our natural skills which, as they may not always require a huge effort, we can assume are less worthy, or that everyone finds them easy. However, this is not the case. By acknowledging and giving life to your passion, you'll naturally find yourself in your flow and you may be amazed at the opportunities that appear both inside and outside of the work place.

Passion-finding Exercise

- Find a photograph of yourself as a child.

- Take some time to connect with the image – breathing slowly.

- Close your eyes and take yourself back to a time in your childhood when you were content and happy.

- Don't worry if you don't see visual images – you may just get a sense or feeling of being a child around this time.

- What were you doing? What were you looking forward to doing?

- When you are ready, open your eyes and write a letter to yourself starting with your name:

- Dear xx, I really want you to know that…

- Start your last paragraph with "And this can be part of your current work by …"

Sometimes, reconnecting with the things that made us happy as children can lead to regaining that joy in adulthood. It doesn't matter what it was!

Be Present

One of the biggest challenges to being in the flow is being 'present'. Being in the here and now, rather than living in the past or the future takes discipline. While there is, of course, a lot to learn from the past and planning for the future is invaluable, unless we are grounded in reality then we're missing opportunities and all the riches that surround us. I've been guilty of living in the future, especially once I had found the vision of the business that I wanted to create. Rather than being in the moment, I wanted to be in the future running my clinic, which seemed a long way from where I was at the time, as there was training, exams and a lot of experience that I needed to go through before I was ready. All the time, I was trying to run, before I could walk: I was resisting my reality and creating struggle in my life. Not only was it exhausting, I was constantly judging myself and others while always trying to move on to the next 'task'.

It's not always easy to be okay in the moment, accepting where we are in life, yet when we don't we make our lives so much harder. My 'tipping point' came from someone saying that it takes two years to set up a business. I just didn't want to hear this, yet after a day or so of feeling (very) cross and angry, I realised I had a choice: I could accept that building a business takes time or I could keep pushing, and living in the future in a way that I used to when working in public relations. I chose the first option as underneath my crossness, my main priority was creating a business that encompassed positive energy and radiated wellbeing and harmony - something that could only happen if *I* was in the present moment. It didn't mean that I stopped focusing on the work, it just meant that I started my day from a place of acceptance of where I was with my vision. I stopped judging myself for not knowing everything and enjoyed the learning experience from a place of ease rather than resentment. It also opened many more doors for me, as being present allowed me to truly connect with others and share my vision of what I wanted to create.

Be On Your Side

Another cause of struggle is when we're not on our own side. This is really important, especially in the office when life can throw us a 'curved ball' and unless we're careful, it can be easy to blame ourselves for making wrong decisions. When I first started working in massage, I used to work in a business each week doing specialised de-stress massage. I loved going there and in the early days the regular money was really useful. However out of the blue, I received an email saying that they didn't need me anymore. I was shocked and immediately blamed myself for this change, thinking that my massage wasn't good enough, or that I was charging too much or generally that I was doing something wrong. I found out a bit later that they had to make a lot of redundancies that week and ultimately the company went into liquidation a few months later; however when I first read that email I became my own worst enemy and rather than being in the flow, I got stuck in a stagnant pool of self-recrimination.

To create a life of ease as opposed to struggle, we need to ensure that we're dedicated to being on our side: our own champion regardless of the circumstances. To take this essential practice on, we need to create a strong and nurturing relationship with ourselves so that when we are tested, we don't crumble and fall back into self-recrimination and blame.

A Date With Myself

Often we can get so busy that there can be times that we forget who we are. Creating time alone is a great way to reconnect with our core selves. It's a similar situation to when we meet someone new and want to find out more about them: we can use time alone as an opportunity to find out more about ourselves and enjoy our own company. To make our own 'date', the only requirement is that you plan something that you really want to do and that you do it alone. My last date with myself was going to a great wood (which is aptly named Great Wood) close to where I live. For me, it was something I really wanted to do, as I love spending time in nature, especially being around trees. When I'm on my own I can spend as long as I want just looking at them and I'm sure I'd probably be hugging trees too if there weren't so many dog walkers around. I get to see the wood so differently when I'm alone. It's still a lovely walk when I with others but when I'm deliberately there just with myself, the whole experience is different.

My next date that I have planned is going to The Sanctuary Spa in Covent Garden. I've planned treatments, lunch and even the train times so that I can enjoy the whole experience of just being with myself. Since I started creating slots in my life for 'Dates With Myself', I've found that I have a stronger relationship and understanding of who I am. I find it easier to stay on my side when faced with challenging circumstances. I know that most issues are caused by misunderstandings and as I know I would not ever deliberately hurt anyone else, I don't feel the need to justify myself so much. Instead, I can rectify issues more simply without making myself or others 'wrong' in the process.

Positive Mental Attitude

> "Your mental attitude is something you can control outright and you must use self-discipline – your mental attitude attracts to you everything that makes you what you are."

Another barrier to being in the flow is the fear of the future and seeing the world through a negative mental attitude. We only have to turn on the TV and we're inundated with doom-ridden messages about the environment, the economy, poverty… I could go on. However, while we all know that we *should* cultivate a positive mental attitude, it's not always easy when we're surrounded by images and messages that can be at best stress triggers, and at worst excuses to stagnate and give up. I can have days when I bounce out of bed and before I know it I've stumbled in the face of negativity be it an unwelcome email, seeing the news headlines or just being in the company of someone particularly draining.

Well at this point, we have to acknowledge that having a positive mental attitude does require effort. It's not always easy, yet once we accept that then it becomes much less of a struggle. Napoleon Hill who first came up with this concept in 1937 said, "Your mental attitude is something you can control outright and you must use self-discipline – your mental attitude attracts to you everything that makes you what you are." So, even if we are surrounded by a sea of pessimists, if we can be strong and make an effort to focus on the positives then the negatives seems to naturally fall away.

This idea was reinforced by a lecture I went to by Roger James Hamilton, the creator of Wealth Dynamics. One of the points he made was that often, we waste our energy worrying about 'old issues', be that global threats or personal difficulties, when we should actually be aware of where we want to be in the future and focus our time and resources on creating that solution right now.

The example he used was 'The Great Manure Crisis' of 1894. In the 19th century, cities depended on horses to survive as they were the major source of transportation. In 1900, London had 11,000 horse drawn cabs; on top of this there were several thousand buses each of which required 12 horses per day. In addition to the thousands of horses required to keep London moving, there were also countless carts, drays, and wains, all continually working to deliver goods which were needed by the rapidly growing population of London. The great problem that worried people incessantly was the amount of manure produced by these horses.

In 1894, *The Times* reported that in 50 years every street in London would be buried under nine feet of manure. Not only that, but as the number of horses grew, people surmised that even more land would need to be devoted to producing hay to feed them (rather than producing food for people), and this too had to be brought into cities and distributed by horse-drawn vehicles. For many people it seemed that urban civilization was doomed.

Yet the issue of drowning in horse manure, a very real fear for our ancestors of the 1900s, naturally fell away as the world evolved and cars were introduced. Global warming is just one example that can send us into a negative state of mind. Yet it was only forty years ago that we were preparing for global cooling and the threat this coming ice age would cause to the human race. While I'm certainly not saying that we should bury our heads in the sand and ignore any uncomfortable issues, we should try to maintain positivity and to stay in the flow, and acknowledge that we do not know all there is to know about any given situation. We need to make time to step out and observe the bigger picture to see what and where we want to focus our energy on rather than feeling overwhelmed with all of the world's problems.

The media and fear-mongers among us seem to relish creating a sense of doom and disempowerment which, if we believe their words, can keep us attached to the problem rather than creating solutions. I was advised several years ago by a successful businessman to stop watching the news or reading the newspapers. If the person was not so successful, I would have been quick to dismiss his comments believing that I needed the news to stay informed and up to date about the world. Yet he argued that by focusing on the news, we'll always be told what is important rather than finding out for ourselves. If we stop dwelling on the problems portrayed by the media we can free up our energy and time to focus on the important things that *we* want to create in our life. I now don't watch the news and rarely read newspapers and find that, like the businessman said, I don't miss anything that is important. I use the additional time to read biographies of inspirational people, follow them on Twitter and focus on my legacy: what I can achieve in my life, rather than all the issues and problems that can stop me.

As The Great Manure Crisis showed, many things that we negatively focus on never happen. Our world is constantly evolving and by staying positive we can shape a positive future. Although there are things outside of our control, as Napolean Hill said, our mental attitude is often the only thing that we can control.

One of my favourite quotes is from Mark Twain who said, "I have been through some terrible things in my life, some of which actually happened". Many of our biggest fears inside and outside of the workplace will never materialise. And yes, of course, tough things do happen but we always have a choice: we can spend our time worrying about them just incase our worst reality is manifested, or we can spend our time in the flow of life, harvesting a positive mental attitude while staying open to all the opportunities, lessons and learnings that life has to offer.

Gratitude

The last point in this chapter is about being grateful. When we appreciate what we have in our life, it immediately puts us in the flow. Being alive today is such a privilege, it's so easy to overlook everything that we have and focus on what we want or don't have in our lives. However, often it can be the things that we don't initially want that can have the most transforming effect upon us, so it's important that we are grateful for the events and people that don't make life easy for us.

During a particularly challenging time in my life, I made sure that before I went to sleep each night I would find three things, from the day, that I was grateful for. And while I was emotionally on my knees, I could always find three things. Just doing this each night lifted my whole spirit as I could see that life was balanced, that it wasn't all one sided and as dark as my day had felt, I knew that tomorrow contained at least three things that I could look forward to. When we're upset, being grateful for the experience is very powerful, even if we can't see the gratitude or the benefit at the time, just knowing that it will move you forward in some way can be enough.

Saying 'Thank You' is an important thing. Meister Eckhart says "If I only had one prayer, it would be 'Thank you'." Dr John F Demartini in *From Stress To Success In Just 31 Days* says that truly successful people are grateful people, as they understand that each event in life should be acknowledged and appreciated. Writing 'Thank You' letters not only creates more gratitude in your life, but also transforms the day of the recipient. With so much technology, emails and texts can often be used as a way to thank someone, but taking time to hand-write a heartfelt message of thanks is one of the best ways that we can manifest gratitude in our life.

Visulisation Exercise

- Close your eyes and take three deep breaths:

- Imagine that you are on a staircase. Start walking up the stairs.

- On each side of the staircase, you can see doors. When you are ready open a door that you are drawn to.

- In the room you see yourself ten years on from now.

- Connect with your future self. What wisdom or advice do you wish to impart to your younger self?

- Use this exercise any time you have a decision to make and are unsure which direction to take. You can specify whatever age you wish to meet your future self by setting that intention at the beginning of the visulisation.

A Few Of My Favourite Things

So as we come towards the end of our time together, I wanted to include some of my favourite products that help me stay cool, calm and collected. We are so lucky that through the Internet, we are able to access, with ease, such a wide variety of knowledge and items. I am hugely grateful for the interconnected world that we live in that makes this possible.

Australian Bush Flower Essences - Space Clearing Mist: This is one to keep on your desk! It's great to use when you are surrounded by stressed colleagues as it is designed to purify and cleanse any negativity. It's incredibly refreshing and uplifting.
0207 703 5550
www.baldwins.co.uk

Cytoplan: Vitamins are a huge topic in themselves and I often blog about them (www.pruenichols.com/blog). One of the problems is that many vitamins out there are of very poor quality, often manufactured in chemical laboratories in China. Cytoplan is a world away from this as it is a highly ethical company that produces whole food and food-state vitamins that the body can readily absorb. In a nutshell, their vitamins and minerals really work and (along with a good diet) can help you stay healthy within the office environment.
01684 310099
www.cytoplan.co.uk

Dr Christiane Northrup: Dr Northrup's first book *Women's Bodies, Women's Wisdom* made a huge impact on me when I first read it many years ago and it's been my health bible every since. All her books are hugely empowering and her website has regular blogs - well worth a look.
www.drnorthrup.com

Epsom Salts: I'm a big advocate of Epsom salt baths. I regularly submerge myself into a warming and nurturing salt bath as it makes me feel calm and relaxed. As Epsom salts contains magnesium (which relaxes our muscles), a twenty-minute soak in two cups of Epsom salts is one of the best ways to release tension after a long day in the office. As it detoxifies as well, you may notice that you feel quite hot afterwards. While I don't mind this, a simple remedy is to have a cold shower after your bath.
0207 703 5550
www.baldwins.co.uk

Healing Herbs Bach Flower Remedies: Rescue Remedy has been a staple product in my life since I was a child. This tincture works on our emotional state and helps to bring calm in times of panic and stress. Along with the space clearing mist, it's well worth keeping a bottle of this in your desk. Just put two drops straight onto your tongue or dilute in water. Although there are many different brands out there, I prefer Healing Herbs as they are the closest to how Dr Bach made the original remedies in the 1930s.
01873 890 218
www.healingherbs.co.uk

Juicing: I bought a juicer many years ago and it sat in my kitchen for a year before it ended up at the back of my cupboard. It was only after a visit to Agape Cottage that I actually started to use it. I now use my juicer every day and can't imagine life without it. Not only do the juices taste delicious but they are one of the best forms of nutrition that we can take. Taking a juice into work is a great boost at 11am and 4pm when your blood sugar tends to drop. The Joe Cross film 'Fat, Sick and Nearly Dead' is great to watch if you have yet to enter the world of juicing. Jason Vale (The Juice Master) is brilliant - he makes it all very simple and very easy.
www.juicemaster.com

Moon Time by Thomas Poppe and Johanna Paungger: This is such a lovely book which describes the power of the moon and how it effects us on earth. I keep this book by my desk.
www.paungger-poppe.com

Origins 'Piece of Mind' tincture: I'm a great fan of Origins and their Piece of Mind tincture is one of my very favourite products. Small enough to fit into any handbag, this little 'on the spot relief' ointment is designed to be rubbed into the temples, head and neck in times of need. It works!
0800 054 2888
www.origins.co.uk

Potatoes Not Prozac by Kathleen Desmaisons: This book is brilliant. Having worked for many years with alcoholics, Ms Desmaisons realised there is a large percentage of people who are dramatically effected by sugar as their biochemistry is wired to respond to sugar as a drug. She explains why for some people sugar is so addictive, and her tone throughout the book is empathetic and kind. There is no Gillian McKeith - you are what you eat – type of judgment here.
www.radiantrecovery.com

Rose Facial Oil, Neal's Yard: While there are many excellent facial oils currently available, this one stands out for its quality and heavenly smell. I use it as part of my signature 'Winter Warmer' massage and always love including this product when I'm working with clients. This is great to use on yourself before you go to bed.
0845 262 3145
www.nealsyardremedies.com

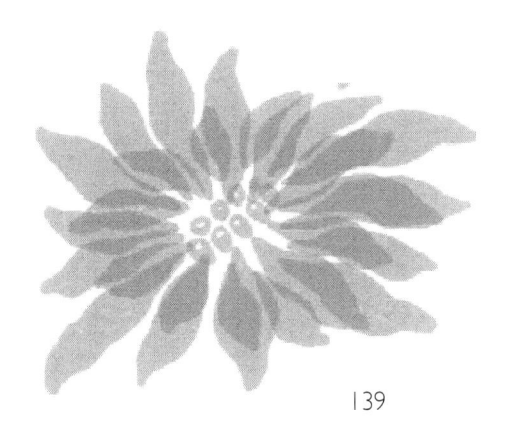

Smudging: Both houses and offices over time can build up negative energy. Smudging is a Native American tradition that burns different herbs to cleanse and purify any negative and stagnant energy. While this ancient tradition may sound intimidating, it's actually very simple and requires a clear intention and a smudge stick. There are many different types of smudge sticks available that are easily available from the Internet. One of my favourites is the Juniper Bundle Smudge Stick that you can buy from Baldwins.
0207 703 5550
www.baldwins.co.uk

Vogel's Milk Thistle Complex tincture: when I'm stressed and have all those toxic stress hormones pumping around my body, my poor liver is forced to work even harder to detoxify my blood. Milk Thistle is like amber nectar for our livers, soothing, regenerating and hugely encouraging. Yes, it's an acquired bitter taste (you put between 15 to 20 drops in water) but I can (almost) hear my liver purring afterwards. Again, worth keeping a bottle in your desk.
0207 703 5550
www.baldwins.co.uk

Your Life of Wellbeing

In this book I have tried to impart some of the lessons I have learned in life – often the hard way – that have led me to understand that we are the masters of our own little universe, and that we can choose to live a healthier, more balanced and creative life.

The 10 Natural Laws I have outlined in this book give guidance and advice about how to eliminate stress, cultivate harmony and follow your heart towards a life of wellbeing. I know from personal experience that it is not always an easy path: but if you stray from the path and fall back into old patterns of behaviour, don't beat yourself up! Just brush yourself down (preferably with a Dry-Skin Brush!), pick yourself up and start all over again. Because ultimately, loving yourself enough to take time for yourself, care about your diet, reduce your stress levels and understand your motivations is the best path to self-realisation.

Take time to find out about the real 'YOU' – and fulfill your potential. You will never look back!

— Prue Nichols June 2014

Bibliography

The 30-Day Fat Burner Diet by Patrick Holford
(Piatkus Books, 1999)

The De-Stress Diet by Charlotte Watts and Anna Magee
(Hay House 2012)

The Energy Equation by Daniel Browne
(Pearson, 2012)

Great Days at Work by Suzanne Hazelton
(Kogan Page 2013)

Healing With Whole Foods by Paul Pitchford
(North Atlantic Books, 2002)

The Hidden Messages in Water by Masaru Emoto
(Atria Books, 2005)

Holistic Anatomy by Pip Waller
(The Dreaming Buttterfly, 2008)

Lean In by Sheryl Sandberg
(Ebury Publishing, 2013)

Medicine Man by Jack Temple
(Findhorn press, 2002)

Men Are From Mars, Women Are From Venus by John Gray
(Harper Paperbacks 2002)

Moon Time by Johanna Paungger and Thomas Peppe
(Random House 2006)

Mother-Daughter Wisdom Dr Christiane Northrup
(Piatkus, 2005)

The Optimum Nutrition Bible by Patrick Holford
(Piatkus 2004)

Prozac Not Potatoes by Dr Kathleen Desmaisons
(Simon & Schuster, 2008)

Psychic Protection: Creating Positive Energies for People and Places by William Bloom
(Piatkus Books, 2009)

The Relaxation Response by Herbert Benson
(HarperTorch, 1976)

Seven Spiritual Laws of Success by Deepak Chopra
(Hay House 2008)

Strong Woman by Karren Brady
(HarperCollins 2013)

The Success Principles by Jack Canfield
(Element, 2005)

Sugar Blues by William Duffy
(Time Warner International, 2002)

The Truth About Stress by Angela Patmore
(Atlantic Books, 2009)

The Tending Instinct by Shelley E Taylor
(Owl Books, 2003)

Turbo-Charge Your Life in 14 Days by Jason Vale
(Thorsons 2005)

You Are What You Eat by Dr Gillian McKeith
(Penguin 2006)

Your Body's Many Cries For Water by Dr Fereydoon Batmanghelidj
(Global Health Solution 2005)

What Really Works by Susan Clark
(Index, 2006)

Women's Bodies, Women's Wisdom by Dr Christiane Northrup
(Bantam 2002)

Stay in Touch

One of the delights of my work is talking to people and hearing their stories about how they manage their stress levels and stay healthy and balanced. It's always fascinating to hear what works (as well as what doesn't!) so please do share your own experiences. I'm also interested in your feedback regarding the book so don't be a stranger - please do stay in touch.

Email: prue@pruenichols.com

Twitter: @pruenichols1

Website: www.pruenichols.com

        www.theorangegrove.net

Blog: www.pruenichols.com/blog

Linked in: uk.linkedin.com/in/pruenichols

Facebook: Prue Nichols

Index

A

adrenal glands	7, 10
adrenaline	6, 7, 33, 44, 46, 87, 89, 91, 94, 102, 103
Agape Cottage	98, 138
agave syrup	41
alcohol	22, 34, 93, 104, 105
allopathic medicine	13
almonds	95
apples - bad	63
artificial sweeteners	39, 103
Arvo Part	96
aspartame	39, 40
astrology	122, 123
Australian Bush Flower Essences	137
autumn	117, 118

B

Batmanghelidj, Dr Fereydoon	20, 21, 25
BBC Radio 4 : Stressed Out broadcast 2000	11
bee breathing	49
being on your side	130
being present	129
blood sugar levels	30, 31, 32, 37, 42
blood sugar rollercoaster	30, 32, 34
Bloom, William	64, 65
boundaries	64, 65
Brady, Karren	
breakfast	37, 38, 105
breath - counting	92
Browne, Daniel	102
bubbles of protection	65
burn out	7, 88, 89

C

caffeine	103
calm breathing	91
Canfield, Jack	66
carbohydrates	31, 32, 34, 37, 38
carob	41
caveman - prehistoric	6
celery	95
central nervous system	49, 87, 88, 103
chamomile	109
Chandola, Professor Tarani	13
Chartered Institute of Personnel and Development 2011 survey	5
children - stress cycle	47
CNBC - Power lunch	3
coffee	22, 27, 35, 101, 103
colds	12, 14, 89, 114
colleagues	16, 58, 59, 60, 61, 63, 66, 67, 70, 71
confrontation	61, 62
Connelly, Dr Dianne	105
constipation	23, 24
conversation - invisible	70
cortisol	6, 7, 87
Cousins, Norman	51, 52
crying	51
Cytoplan	137

D

dancing	55
De Villiers, Jean - Pierre	44
dehydration	16, 17, 19, 20, 22, 23, 24, 28, 88
Demartini, John	135
Desmaisons, Kathleen	34, 139
detox	89, 113, 117, 118
digestive system	12, 13, 14, 23
diuretics	27
Downs, Georgina	94
dry skin brushing	115, 116
Duffy, William	29

E

Eckhart, Meister	135
Einstein, Albert	111
email	62, 73, 74, 80, 81
Embercombe	123
emotions	46, 47, 48
Emoto, Masaru	18
epsom salts	115, 138
Equinox	112, 117, 118
eustress	2
Evander Holyfield	9
Evin prison, Tehran	20
excessive water consumption	26
extroverts	90

F

Facebook	75, 81, 82
fatty acids	31
feet	108
fight or flight	5, 6, 9, 10, 11, 12, 16, 18, 33, 41, 46, 49, 50, 53, 59, 87, 91, 92, 93, 103
five rhythms dancing	55, 56
Frank, Anne	112
frankincense essential oil	93
fructans	41
fructose	41
full moon	120, 121

G

Gallop Business Journal	59
glucogen	30, 31
glucose	30, 31, 33, 37
Glycaemic index	36, 38, 41
gratitude	135
Gray, John	59
great manure crisis	133, 134
gym	43, 44, 48

H

Haas, Elson M	116
Hamilton, Roger James	133
Hazelton, Suzanne	60
headaches	11, 13, 23, 33, 89
Healing Herbs - Bach Flower Remedies	138
heart attack	11
Hill, Napolean	133, 134
hindbrain	9, 46
Holford, Patrick	35
homeostatis	31, 46
honey	41
Hunt, Bridget	37

I

immune system	10, 14, 113, 114, 115
insulin	30, 31, 42
introverts	90

J

juicing	138

K

Kirkman, Sally	122

L

laughing	51, 52
lavender essential oil	93, 107
leisure sickness	89
Lindlahr, Henry	114
liver	31, 105
lunar cycle	119
lymphatic system	115

M

Marchant, Danielle	98
massage	7, 54, 55, 86, 95
McKeith, Gillian	95
melatonin	108

mindset - shifting	66
Moore, Sarra	118
movement	43 - 57, 61, 90
muscles	12, 13, 31, 89
music	96

N

Napolean	102
nature	111 - 124
Neal's Yard	117, 139
new moon	120
New Year resolutions	112
night-time ritual	107
Northrup, Christiane	23, 25, 137

O

Origins - piece of mind	139

P

pancreas	31, 42
parasympathetic system	11
passion finding exercise	128
Pasteur, Louis	114
pausing	8590
Percy pigs	32,
perfectionism	81, 82
pesticides	93, 94, 103
physical action	46
pillow - punching	53, 61
pineal gland	108
pituitary gland	18
planning	78, 79, 80
Poppe, Thomas & Paungger, Johanna	138
positive mental attitude	132, 133, 134, 135
power naps	107, 108
predators - prehistoric	5
prioritising	76, 77, 78
procrastination	73, 74, 75, 76, 78, 81, 83
protein	37

Public Relations	3, 5, 19, 77, 129
Pukka herbal teas	109

R

ranting	52
Red Bull	22
refined sugar	30, 32, 88, 93
reflexology	108
Relaxation Response - Herbert Benson	90
REM	104
Reptilian shadow	9, 46, 53, 62, 67
rest	7, 8, 14, 44, 86
rest and repair	11, 87
road rage	6, 48
Rohn, Jon	60
rosemary essential oil	93

S

sabre-toothed tiger	6
Sandberg, Sheryl	62, 82
sex drive	6, 12, 18, 95
shaking	50
siesta	108
sleep	88, 100 - 110
sleep debt	101
sleep patterns	7, 102, 104, 116, 119
sleep stages	104, 107
sleeping pills	105
slow breathing	49
smudging	140
solar/lunar teas	117
spring	112 - 115
stress	2-15, 16, 35, 58, 74, 83
stress Animal - Drowing Duck	69
stress Animal - Lonely Mole	68
stress Animal - Mute Mouse	70
stress Animal - Roaring Lion	67
stress Animal - Scared Deer	68
stress cycle	2, 5, 7, 8, 12, 44, 86

stress response	9, 10, 87, 94
sugar	29 - 42
sugar cane	29
summer	116, 117
summer solstice	116
sweating	7, 13, 33, 35
sympathetic system	11

T

talking	53, 54
Tantrum Club	47
Taylor, Shelley E	59
television	57, 85, 106
Temple, Jack	94
Theron, Adele	47
thirst pains	23, 25
touch	95, 96
Tracy, Brian	76
Twain, Mark	76, 80, 134
Tyson, Mike	9

U

urine	24

V

vacuum cleaning - vigorous	53, 61
Vale, Jason	138
valerian	109
vending machine	33, 34, 43, 44
Viridian	109
vitamin C	51
Vogel's milk thistle complex	140

W

walking	50, 55, 57
Waller, Pip	51, 101
waning moon	121
water	16 - 28, 16, 17, 18, 19, 21, 88
water retention	18

Watts, Charlotte & Magee, Anna	95
waxing moon	120
WC/toilet	22, 49, 50
winter	118, 119
winter solstice	118
Work Foundation's Stress at Work report	13

Y

yoga	56

Printed in Great Britain
by Amazon.co.uk, Ltd.,
Marston Gate.